Black Box

BLACK BOX

KAL 007 and the Superpowers

Alexander Dallin

University of California Press

Berkeley   Los Angeles   London

University of California Press
Berkeley and Los Angeles, California
University of California Press, Ltd.
London, England
©1985 by
The Regents of the University of California
Printed in the United States of America

1   2   3   4   5   6   7   8   9

Library of Congress Cataloging in Publication Data
Dallin, Alexander.
    Black box.
    Bibliography: p.
    Includes index.
    1. Korean Air Lines Incident, 1983.
2. United States—Foreign relations—Soviet Union.
3. Soviet Union—Foreign relations—United States.
4. Airspace (International law) I. Title.
E183.8.S65D34   1985   909'.096454   84-24151
ISBN 0-520-05515-2

To Andy, Linda, and Tasha

Contents

Preface   ix
List of Abbreviations   xii

1.   **September 1983**   1

    The Crash   1
    The Context   4
    The Crisis Deepens   6
    Charges, Confessions, Corrections   11
    The Flight Replayed   17

2.   **How and Why: Explications and Explanations I**   26

    Why Did KAL 007 Stray?   26
      The Innocent Versions   27
      Mysterious Mission?   40
      If So, Why?   48

3.   **How and Why: Explications and Explanations II**   57

    Why Did the Su-15 Do It?   57
      Identification and Interception   58
      Excursus I: Law and Custom   66
      History and Context   69
      The Superpowers Face-to-Face   74
      Excursus II: Precedents and Analogs   79
      Political and Bureaucratic Culture   82
      Guesses and Gaffes   84

4.   Consequences and Conclusions   88

Handling the Crisis   89
Crisis Management and Learning   95
Perceptions and Politics   100

Notes   107
Bibliography   123
Index   127

Preface

This study was undertaken in pursuit of several objectives. The most obvious was the attempt to reconstruct the events of September 1983 when the Soviet downing of a civilian airliner, Korean Air Lines flight 007, with its 269 victims, provoked an international crisis of the first order.

There were then—and there remain now—many unknowns, many strands of contradictory and incompatible evidence and allegations, and many hypotheses about causes and circumstances that can be neither validated nor falsified. The loss of the "black box" in the plane's wreckage makes it impossible to test some of these surmises conclusively. One further purpose of this effort, then, was to attempt a systematic review of the various hypotheses—voiced at the time or articulated later—regarding the behavior of KAL 007, the Soviet Air Defense Command, and, insofar as it was relevant, agencies of the United States. In the aftermath of the tragedy, a number of extreme and wildly implausible explanations were generated on all sides. It may be instructive to learn how a careful analysis of the available information—incomplete, alas, as it is—permits discarding certain surmises as groundless, questioning some as incompatible with known facts, and setting aside others as highly implausible. I do not claim to have put all the pieces of this fascinating puzzle together in any definitive fashion, but I hope that I have succeeded in narrowing the range of possibly sound and tenable explanations to a minimum.

Still more importantly, the incident provides the raw material for a case study of how both superpowers behaved in a (presumably unexpected) crisis situation. Questions may properly be raised concerning the decision-making at both ends as well as the public handling of the crisis by the two superpowers. Both on the Soviet and on the American side, the behavior evidenced under the circumstances is bound to reflect certain cultural, institutional, and perhaps ideological characteristics. In particular, in facing a "black box" situation in which analysts and decision-makers of both powers had incomplete and partially unreliable information to work with, they had to fall back on prior assumptions and latent prejudices, which were bound to become manifest more clearly than they would have under other conditions. In turn, the experience also suggests some lessons regarding the supoerpowers' larger pattern of behavior in the managing of international crises.

After the initial attention which the incident had, understandably, attracted in September 1983, there was a new flurry of interest in the summer of 1984, leading up to the event's first anniversary. A number of new publications appeared—in Canada, England, Japan, and elsewhere—and papers dealing with variant hypotheses made their appearance in scholarly journals as well as in popular or even sensational media. These publications testified to the challenges which the case presented to the analyst; with a few exceptions, they did not materially add to the pool of factual data, but some of their speculation served to broaden the range of alternatives that needed to be given earnest consideration.

To the analyst, one frustrating circumstance is, of course, the surmise that there may well be files, somewhere behind locked doors and in classified cabinets, which would help answer some of the key questions that remain in dispute, as well as participant-observers who could help shed some further light. I can only hope that, with time, all such sources will become available to responsible scholars and journalists, but that in the meanwhile this effort will have contributed to the process of understanding both the events and their background.

I thank all those who helped me gather and interpret the information for this study. I am grateful for the senior fellowship awarded me by the W. Averell Harriman Institute at Columbia University which made the research possible, and for the encouragement provided by its faculty and staff, and particularly its director, Marshall D. Shulman. I am happy to acknowledge the conscientious research assistance of Kristen Benson, who also helped prepare the maps, Lieza Champlin, and Denis M. Mc-Cauley. I am partiularly indebted to Edmund Levin, who repeatedly found sources whose existence I did not even suspect.

I benefited substantially from my discussions with some colleagues and from comments by others who read drafts of this manuscript. They include, in particular, Barton Bernstein, Alexander George, David Holloway, Robert Legvold, Stephen Meyer, and Cynthia Roberts. Several others were very helpful by correspondence. None of the above, of course, have any responsibility for the results. Still others, in and out of the government, generously shared their knowledge or offered their opinions without wishing to be identified. This includes a series of interviews I was able to conduct in Washington and in Moscow in the summer of 1984. Several persons shared manuscripts and papers with me, for which I am grateful: I learned something from all of them, whether or not I agreed with their conclusions. I also appreciate the assistance of the staff of the International Civil Aviation Organization in Montreal. Finally, the work would have been neither undertaken nor completed without the advice, critique, and support of Gail Warshofsky Lapidus. Let this be a token of my gratitude.

Alexander Dallin
September 1984

Abbreviations

ACC	Area Control Center
AFS	Aeronautical fixed service
AFTN	Aeronautical Fixed Telecommunications Network
AIP	Aeronautical Information Publication
AMS	Aeronautical mobile service
ANO	[Russian for] Aeronavigational Lights
ARTCC	Air Route Traffic Control Center
ATC	Air Traffic Control
ATS	Air Traffic Service
FIR	Flight Information Region
IFF	Identification/Friend or Foe?
IFSS	International Flight Service Station
INS	Inertial Navigational System
KAL	Korean Air Lines
KGB	[Russian for] Committee of State Security
LTT	Landline Teletypewriter
MBFR	Mutual and Balanced Force Reduction
MHz	MegaHertz
PVO	Protivo-vozdushnaia oborona [Anti-air defense command]
RCAG	Remote-control air-ground communications facility
SAR	Search and Rescue
SLBM	Submarine-launched ballistic missile
SSR	Secondary Surveillance Radar
VHF	Very high frequency
VOR	VHF Omni-bearing range radio station

1

September 1983

Forty-four years, to the day, after World War II had broken out, the world stumbled into another crisis whose dimensions were at first hard to gauge. For newspaper readers and television audiences in the West, it began with an ambiguous dispatch. A South Korean airliner on a flight from New York, with a stop at Anchorage, Alaska, scheduled to land in Seoul, South Korea, at 5:53 A.M. on September 1 (4:53 P.M. Eastern Daylight Time [EDT], or 2053 hours Greenwich Mean Time [GMT]), had failed to arrive and had not been heard from for some time.*

The Crash

At first, details were sketchy and confusion reigned. Civilian air controllers at Narita, Tokyo's international airport, had last heard from the plane at 3:23 A.M., when it reported its location as 113 miles south of Nemuro at the eastern tip of Hokkaido, the northernmost of the islands that make up Japan. According to the Associated Press, representatives of the Japanese Air Force stated that its radar had never picked up the jetliner—a Boeing 747—at the location where the plan had claimed to be.

Korean Air Lines (KAL) officials in Seoul, perhaps seeking to reassure the waiting friends and relatives of the passengers, stated more than seven

---

*To avoid confusion, times will hereafter be given in Greenwich Mean Time (GMT) unless otherwise indicated. The following table of the time zones involved may be helpful:

GMT	Moscow Summer Time	Japan/Korea Summer Time	Sakhalin Time	Kamchatka Time	EDT (U.S.)
1500	1900	2400	0300	0400	1100

hours later that the aircraft might have been forced by Soviet air force planes to land on the island of Sakhalin, a part of the Soviet Union off limits to foreign commercial aircraft. According to the *New York Times,* the Korean Foreign ministry gave the American Central Intelligence Agency (CIA) as its source for this story. In Washington, a spokesperson for the CIA would "neither confirm nor deny" the report. Evidently, Japanese military radar had tracked a plane, surrounded by others close by and then suddenly disappearing from their radar screens, "flying near Sakhalin" just a few minutes after the Korean jet had checked into Narita by radio, reporting its position to be hundreds of miles away. Another airline official speculated that the plane might have exploded in midair.[1] In any event, the same version—that the plane was down and apparently the passengers were safe—was initially also passed out by the State Department in Washington to relatives of passengers who had been on the plane.

The first public Soviet reaction came in a brief report from TASS International Service over Moscow radio (0605 GMT):

> Tokyo, September 1 (TASS)—A South Korean Boeing 747 passenger plane on a regular flight from New York to Seoul has disappeared without trace. On board were 269 passengers and crew. The last time the plane was in contact was 80 km east of Hokkaido. Searches mounted by Japanese authorities produced no result.

This item was repeated over the air several times during the following hours. At about the same time, the Japanese news agency Kyodo was able to report more alarming developments from Moscow and Tokyo. First it announced (Tokyo radio in English, 0712 GMT) that officials at Sakhalin's Yuzhno-Sakhalinsk airport in a telephone conversation had denied reports that a South Korean jetliner had landed there. A few hours later, it reported from Moscow (Tokyo radio in English, 1357 GMT):

> The Soviet Union Thursday bluntly denied that the missing South Korean jumbo jet airliner landed on Soviet territory. The denial came when Kazuhiko Togo, counsellor of the Japanese Embassy in Moscow, met with a Soviet Foreign Ministry official at the ministry's offices Thursday morning. Togo said the Soviet official initially said only that the South Korean airliner which went missing earlier Thursday in the sea north of Japan did not land on the Soviet territory. When Togo questioned the official whether this meant the missing South Korean airliner was not in Soviet territory, the official replied that it was not within Soviet territory since it had not landed on Soviet territory, Togo told Japanese newsmen. Japanese Embassy sources said later they could not rule out the possibility the ill-fated South Korean plane was shot down by the Soviet Union.[2]

The same evening (Tokyo time), Kyodo reported that the Japanese Foreign Ministry had summoned the Soviet ambassador to Japan, Vladimir Pavlov, to seek information about the Korean jet. As Yoshiya Kato, director-general of the Bureau of European and Pacific Affairs, told reporters, the jet most likely crashed into the ocean near the southwestern tip of Sakhalin. Reportedly, Pavlov spoke of an "anti-Soviet campaign" launched by the Japanese media in connection with the plane's disappearance and called reports that the plane might have been shot down by Soviet aircraft an unfriendly comment.[3]

Finally, at 9:07 P.M. Moscow time (1707 GMT)—almost twenty-four hours after the incident—TASS issued an official statement:

> An unidentified plane entered the airspace of the Soviet Union over the Kamchatka Peninsula from the direction of the Pacific Ocean and then for the second time violated the airspace of the USSR over Sakhalin Island on the night from August 31 to September 1. The plane did not have [aerial navigation] lights [on], did not respond to queries and did not enter into [radio] contact with the dispatcher [air traffic ground control] service.
> Fighters of the anti-aircraft defense [Air Defense Command] which were sent aloft towards the intruder plane tried to give it assistance in directing it to the nearest airfield. But the intruder plane did not react to the signals and warnings from the Soviet fighters and continued its flight in the direction of the Sea of Japan.[4]

American diplomats, it was revealed, had also been in touch with their Soviet opposite numbers. Late on August 31, Washington time (EDT), Assistant Secretary of State for European Affairs Richard Burt telephoned the Soviet chargé d'affaires, Oleg Sokolov, who professed to have no information about the plane. In Moscow, U.S. chargé Warren Zimmerman raised the question with Aleksandr Bessmertnykh, of the Soviet foreign ministry, to no avail. Apparently, the foreign office genuinely knew nothing of the whole affair. Early the next morning, Under Secretary of State Lawrence Eagleburger called in Sokolov for another futile round. But Soviet Foreign Minister Andrei Gromyko, it was later revealed, had meanwhile sent a message to Secretary of State George P. Shultz along the lines of the TASS statement, but adding that Soviet search planes had found "signs of a possible crash" near Moneron (Kaiba) Island, some thirty-five miles off southwest Sakhalin—a message which the State Department's spokesperson declared to be a "totally inadequate" response, while reiterating the U.S. demand for a "satisfactory explanation."[5]

The United States government decided to wait no longer. At a press conference the same morning, an uncharacteristically angry Secretary

Shultz laid out the Administration's version of the events. The United States had evidence—presumably from electronic monitoring of Soviet communications—that Soviet radar had tracked the South Korean jet, Korean Air Lines flight 007, for about two and one-half hours while it "strayed into Soviet airspace over the Kamchatka Peninsula and over the Sea of Okhotsk and over the Sakhalin Islands [*sic*]."

> A Soviet pilot [the Secretary continued] reported visual contact with the aircraft at 1812 hours [GMT, i.e., 0312 Tokyo/Seoul time]. The Soviet plane was, we know, in constant contact with its ground control. At 1821 hours the Korean aircraft was reported by the Soviet pilot at 10,000 meters. At 1826 hours the Soviet pilot reported that he fired a missile and the target was destroyed. At 1830 hours the Korean aircraft was reported by radar at 5,000 meters. At 1838 hours the Korean plane disappeared from the radar screen.
>
> We know that at least eight Soviet fighters reacted at one time or another to the airliner. The pilot who shot the airliner down reported after the attack that he had in fact fired a missile, that he had destroyed the target and that he was breaking away.

Reporting that the United States had expressed its "grave concern over the shooting down of an unarmed civilian plane," Shultz added: "The United States reacts with revulsion to this attack. Loss of life appears to be heavy. We can see no excuse whatsoever for this appalling act."

The Context

The late summer of 1983 was widely seen as a propitious time to move toward repairing a seriously damaged Soviet-American relationship.

After the Soviet-American honeymoon ushered in by the Nixon-Kissinger visit to Moscow in 1972, the conclusion of SALT I, and a variety of joint activities which reflected and in turn promoted the spirit of détente, superpower relations from the mid-1970s on had experienced a serious decline, with the Jackson-Vanik Amendment, on the one hand, and Soviet proxy intervention in Angola, on the other, symbolizing the growing tension and the failure of superpower cooperation. The pattern reverted to a sequence of unilateral and increasingly adversarial moves and, on both sides, a heightened suspicion of the other's motives. Dramatizing this process, the Soviet invasion of Afghanistan in 1979–80 led to sanctions and counteractions by the Carter Administration, including an abandonment of efforts to have the U.S. Senate ratify the SALT II treaty and a withdrawal from the Olympic games about to be held in Moscow.

The election of Ronald Reagan in November 1980 brought to power some of the most ideological and vigorously anti-communist officials ever to preside in Washington, but in practice the Reagan Administration drifted between rhetorical confrontation with the Soviet Union and a massive buildup of U.S. military capabilities, on the one hand, and, on the other, efforts seemingly aimed at finding a modus vivendi, especially in such areas as the deployment of nuclear weapons and arms control, which were of concern to public opinion at home and in Allied countries abroad.[6] Still, official American hostility to the Soviet Union reached new heights and was matched by no less vitriolic Soviet rhetoric about the Reagan regime.

Oddly, there was an element of tentativeness and uncertainty at both ends of the Soviet-American relationship. It was as if neither power had a clear strategy of how to deal with the other. In Moscow, where upon Leonid Brezhnev's death in November 1982 Yuri Andropov succeeded to the top position in the Kremlin, Soviet experts seemed to be increasingly inclined to write off all chances of a significant improvement of relations with the Reagan Administration, and some counseled sitting it out until after the presidential election of 1984 in the United States, while avoiding undue risks of confrontation and escalation abroad. In Washington, the Administration's "pragmatist" advocates of a new approach to Moscow finally won the day, in the summer of 1983, over White House and Pentagon opposition, and plans for new rounds of talks and negotiations in a variety of areas were coming to fruition—from a new five-year agreement to sell U.S. grain to the Soviet Union (signed in Moscow on August 25), to the opening of new consulates in Kiev and New York, and negotiating a new cultural and scientific exchange agreement.[7]

Arms-control talks were likewise continuing, with particular attention to intermediate-range nuclear missiles, in view of the impending NATO deployment of U.S. Pershing II and cruise missiles in Western Europe, which was to begin in December. But it was not yet clear whether either side would show enough flexibility, statesmanship, and eagerness to reach an agreement that might forestall the deployment. There is little doubt that Moscow perceived the massive U.S. military buildup launched in the 1980s as a serious challenge and in all likelihood moved, not later than mid-1983, to decisions to counter and offset the anticipated American capability. If this was indeed the case, then September 1983 was just about the latest date at which the new decisions on the Soviet side could be canceled and turned around without undue cost: one more reason why this was perceived to be a critical season in Soviet-American affairs.

In this general atmosphere of tension and mutual hostility, which was widely described as a renewal of the Cold War, third areas tended to be perceived as pawns in the dispute between the superpowers, so that not only Afghanistan but also the crisis over Lebanon and the latent contest over Central America—notably, the suspicion of Soviet-backed reinforcement by Cuba of the Sandinista government and its armed forces, and American aid to Honduras and El Salvador and "covert" support for armed Nicaraguan exile groups—added fuel to the flames of Soviet-American fears, mutual suspicions, and enmities.

It remains entirely uncertain what result the beginning American attempts to break out of the deadlock would have had if these efforts had not been undercut precisely by the events described here. They would not be renewed until the following year, and by then the entire climate of relations had become even more inclement—in no small measure, as a result of the incident we are dealing with here. Meanwhile, the tension tended to be expressed increasingly in terms of what might be labeled superpower body language: a partially unadvertised complex of activities including not only muscle-flexing by symbolic movement of naval vessels, paratroop units, marine detachments, and nuclear submarines, but also extensive mutual monitoring of missile tests, military communications, and troop movements, satellite photography of significant installations and deployments, shadowing of naval vessels by adversary submarines, and virtually incessant air patrol by reconnaissance aircraft of each side. This, plus the increasingly bitter rhetoric, added to the nervousness everywhere, compounded by the jitters generated by growing attempts—especially in Western Europe—to dramatize the potential devastation of a nuclear exchange.

The Crisis Deepens

After an initially casual reaction, President Reagan broke off his vacation at his ranch near Santa Barbara, California, to return to Washington—presumably to meet with the National Security Council and to consider countermeasures—expressing his "revulsion" over this "horrifying act of violence."[8] Statements of indignation came promptly from a number of capitals; protests and demonstrations were organized in front of Soviet offices and residences abroad; and public figures in the United States, South Korea, and Japan called for vigorous reprisals. Clearly, Moscow had to respond to the American charges.

On September 3, *Pravda* carried a new, lengthier TASS statement. Rather than admitting Soviet responsibility for the destruction of the

Korean jet, Moscow launched a counterattack. First, as far as the intruding plane was concerned, it had "deviated from the existing international route in the direction of the Soviet Union's territory by up to 500 kilometers and for more than two hours. . . . In violation of international regulations, the plane was flying without aerial navigation lights, did not respond to radio signals from Soviet air traffic control services, and itself made no attempts to establish such contact." As for the Soviet planes, they "repeatedly tried to establish contact with the plane, using generally accepted signals, and to escort it to the nearest airfield on the Soviet Union's territory. However, the intruder-plane ignored all this. Over the island of Sakhalin, a Soviet plane fired warning shots of tracer shells along its flight path."

As for its disappearance, TASS declared: "Soon after this, the intruder-plane left Soviet airspace and continued its flight toward the Sea of Japan. For approximately ten minutes it was in the observation zone of radar devices, after which it could no longer be observed." Without explicitly denying the Soviet role in the destruction of the airliner, TASS continued to imply Soviet innocence.

In its counterthrust, TASS assailed the "furor" over the plane's fate in the West, and contended, on its part, that there was

> more and more reason to believe that the itinerary and nature of the flight were not accidental. It is indicative that now, after the fact, the American side not only officially admits the fact of that plane's violation of Soviet airspace but also cites data from which it is evident that the relevant American services kept a very close watch on the flight throughout its duration.
>
> One asks: If it was an ordinary flight of a civilian airplane that was under continuous observation, then why were no steps taken by the American side to end the flagrant violation of USSR airspace and return the plane to the international route?
>
> Why did the American authorities, which are now resorting to all kinds of dirty insinuations about the USSR, not try to establish contact with the Soviet side and provide the necessary data about this flight?

Everything considered, the intrusion "cannot be regarded as anything but a preplanned act. The hope [calculation] was [evidently] that special intelligence objectives could be [realized] without hindrance by using civilian planes as a cover." In other words, this was a deliberate *provokatsiia*—a provocation—the term used with considerable repetition in the following days and weeks to describe the incident. "This is also indicated," the statement added, "by the impudent, slanderous statement against the Soviet Union that U.S. President Reagan immediately made."

Finally, "TASS is authorized to state that leading circles of the Soviet Union express regret in connection with the loss of human lives and at the same time resolutely condemn those who, consciously or as a result of criminal negligence, have allowed people to die and are now trying to use what happened for unscrupulous political purposes."[9]

Upon his return to Washington, Reagan had met with the National Security Council the evening of September 2, and the next day made a public broadcast marked by bluntness:

> I want to speak to you briefly about the recent act of brutality that continues to horrify us all. I am referring to the outrageous Soviet attack against 269 people aboard the unarmed Korean passenger plane. This murder of innocent civilians is a serious international issue between the Soviet Union and civilized people everywhere who cherish individual rights and value human life.

Indicating that the U.S., along with others, was about to raise the matter in the United Nations Security Council, Reagan continued: "The evidence is clear. It leaves no doubt. It is time for the Soviets to account. The Soviet Union owes the world the fullest possible explanation and apology for their inexcusable act of brutality. So far they have flunked the test. Even now they continue to distort and deny the truth." He would not refrain from drawing a more sweeping lesson:

> People everywhere could draw only one conclusion from their violent behavior: There is a glaring gap between Soviet words and deeds. They speak endlessly about their love of brotherhood, disarmament and peace. But they reserve the right to disregard aviation safety and to sacrifice human lives.

Whereas Moscow had reminded its audience that this was not the first American-sponsored violation of Soviet airspace, Reagan replied:

> Make no mistake on this last point. This is not the first time the Soviets have shot at and hit a civilian airliner when it flew over Soviet territory. Our government does not shoot down foreign aircraft over U.S. territory even though commercial aircraft from the Soviet Union and Cuba have overflown sensitive U.S. military facilities. We and other civilized countries follow procedures to prevent a tragedy rather than to provoke one. But while the Soviets accuse others of wanting to return to the Cold War, it is they who have never left it behind.[10]

Thus the verbal vituperation was being stepped up, while the gulf between the Soviet and American versions continued to grow.

If the facts in the case, as they became known, seemed to present Moscow with a serious embarrassment, the United States suffered at least a minor setback when word leaked out from a briefing of Congressional leaders on September 4, later officially confirmed, that when Soviet radar had first spotted the Korean jet, there was also an American "spy plane," an RC-135, in the air and thus on Soviet radar in the same area. Though Washington insisted that by the time KAL 007 was shot down the RC-135 had long returned to its base in the Aleutian Islands, the official U.S. statement about the high-speed reconnaissance plane acknowledged that it had at one point flown within seventy-five miles of KAL 007 and had in fact crossed its path, and that when the Korean jet was over Kamchatka (the U.S. claimed to know), "it was initially identified by the Soviets as an RC-135 and then as an unidentified aircraft." The U.S. government position was, however, that the two aircraft are entirely different in shape and size and there could have been no actual confusion, especially since Soviet fighter planes had had extensive "visual contact" with the passenger airliner before it was shot down.[11]

Meanwhile, the Soviet side, too, had had time to piece together a somewhat more elaborate story. Still stopping well short of an explicit acknowledgment that a Soviet plane had shot the jet down, *Pravda* on September 5 published an article entitled "Political Provocation With Far-Reaching Aims," by Colonel General Semion F. Romanov, Chief of Staff of the Air Defense Forces (which appeared in the form of an interview with Romanov in *Krasnaia Zvezda,* the armed forces newspaper, the following day). The intruder-plane, he argued, had not responded either to the standard radio call signal or to other internationally accepted techniques by Soviet interceptors of warning other planes, such as rocking one's wings and blinking one's lights. "Having used all possibilities of attracting attention and escorting the intruder-plane out of our sovereign airspace, the pilot of our interceptor fired warning shots, using tracer shells, along the path of the intruder-plane, in yet another effort to draw the attention of the intruder-plane's crew to the flagrant violation of our airspace." General Romanov continued: "In the West a great deal of noise is being made to the effect that the Soviet pilot knew very well that he was dealing with a civilian airplane. But this is just what the Soviet pilot didn't know." Moreover, the intruder-plane was allegedly flying with its lights out. Romanov went on to list a number of alleged violations of Soviet airspace by American planes, all of which were part of the same pattern of "authorized provocations."[12] Other Soviet media wasted no time in painting an elaborate scenario of American intelligence activities and "provocations" into which the flight of KAL 007 allegedly fitted perfectly.

On the American side, the verbal escalation reached its peak with President Reagan's address to the nation on September 5 and with Ambassador Jeane Kirkpatrick's presentation of the case before the United Nations Security Council on September 6. Only later did it become known that these statements were preceded by high-level arguments in Washington on how most appropriately to respond to the downing of KAL 007. While the words remained strong, it was actually the more moderate orientation in the White House, the National Security Council, and the State Department that prevailed—largely because of the President's own preference—over those who had pressed for more drastic action. Thus, Defense Secretary Caspar Weinberger had proposed suspending some of the ongoing arms-control negotiations with Moscow. "Most hardliners," columnists Evans and Novak reported, their own preferences showing, "are outraged. Passivity, they believe, will encourage Soviet misbehavior. . . . Words used to us [to describe Administration policy] by a variety of such national security experts include 'atrocious,' 'disastrous,' 'embarrassing' and 'demeaning.'"[13] But they protested in vain.

In his television address, Reagan spoke of the "Korean airline massacre" as a "crime against humanity" which "must never be forgotten, here or throughout the world." The President proclaimed: "Let me state as plainly as I can: there was absolutely no justification, either legal or moral, for what the Soviets did." As for the cause of the Boeing 747 flying so far and so long over Soviet territory, despite its advanced technological equipment, "no one will ever know whether a mistake was made in giving the computer the course or whether there was a malfunction." Reagan then proceeded to play two brief segments from the tape of transmissions from Soviet fighters to a Soviet ground station, clearly indicating that one of the fighters had launched a missile and reported the "target"—the Korean jet—to have been destroyed. The United States thereby confirmed what had been only surmise: that it had evidence of Soviet culpability, which undercut the Soviet posture of silence or denial. Reagan declared:

> This was the Soviet Union against the world and the moral precepts which guide human relations among people everywhere. It was an act of barbarism, born of a society which wantonly disregards individual rights and the value of human life and seeks constantly to expand and dominate other nations.

Noting Soviet "harassment" of the Japanese search for wreckage and bodies, he added:

But we shouldn't be surprised by such inhuman brutality. Memories come back of Czechoslovakia, Hungary, Poland, the gassing of villages in Afghanistan. If the massacre and their subsequent conduct are intended to intimidate, they have failed in their purpose. From every corner of the globe the word is defiance in the face of this unspeakable act and defiance of the system which excuses it and tries to cover it up.[14]

Repeating the demand for a Soviet apology, he went on to list a number of retaliatory steps the U.S. was about to take—measures which seemed, to some observers, rather insignificant in comparison both with the "deed" and with the American rhetoric about it.

In addition to seeking reparations from Moscow for the families of the victims, the White House demanded "action to see that this never happens again." Other than pressing for undefined changes in civil aviation procedures, the U.S. response included the closing of offices in the United States of the Soviet airline, Aeroflot (whose flights to U.S. airports had been suspended under the Carter Administration in retaliation for the Soviet invasion of Afghanistan); a suspension of negotiations on several bilateral arrangements, such as the opening of new consulates in Kiev and New York and the renewal of a cultural exchange agreement; a decision to take the matter both to the United Nations Security Council and to the Council of the International Civil Aviation Organization; a request that Congress pass a joint resolution condemning "this Soviet crime" (such a resolution was indeed passed, without dissent, within ten days); and an effort to persuade other countries and pilots' associations to suspend flights to and from the Soviet Union for a specified period of time— say, sixty days (the time adopted in the Canadian suspension of Aeroflot flights into Montreal and also proposed by the governing board of the International Federation of Air Line Pilots Associations, representing pilots of seventeen commercial airlines flying to the Soviet Union). In practice, the ban produced a patchwork of suspensions, boycotts, and terminations by different nations, airlines, and pilots' and ground controllers' associations for varying periods of time. By the end of September, the boycott began to crumble, and most scheduled flights (though not to and from the United States) were soon resumed.

Charges, Confessions, Corrections

The tapes of Soviet intercepts from which Ronald Reagan had included two brief excerpts in his speech constituted the dramatic centerpiece of Ambassador Kirkpatrick's address to the UN Security Council the following day. The Council had begun debating the matter on September 2 and had heard vigorous denunciations of the Soviet action by Canadian, Australian, and other Council members and the South Korean observer, as well as a repetition of the standard TASS version by deputy delegate Richard Ovinnikov. Then, on September 6, the U.S. introduced the tapes, playing the text in Russian with simultaneous translation on the monitoring screens (and offering to make copies available on audio cassettes to any interested delegation).

These tapes, reproduced and discussed below, permitted the U.S. to indicate when Soviet radar had begun tracking the Korean airliner over Sakhalin, how Soviet fighters had tried to intercept it, and what the three fighter pilots had told their ground stations during the final pursuit which led to the jet's destruction. If the tapes were authentic—and there was no serious challenge on that score—there could be no doubt about the intentional destruction of the airliner by a Soviet fighter plane, on instructions from its ground controllers. Mrs. Kirkpatrick continued:

> The transcript that we have just heard needs little explanation. Quite simply, it establishes that the Soviets decided to shoot down a civilian airliner, shot it down, murdering the 269 persons on board, and lied about it. . . . Contrary to what the Soviets have repeatedly stated, the interceptor pilot saw the airliner's navigation lights and reported that fact to the ground on three occasions. Contrary to Soviet statements, the pilot made no mention of firing any warning shots—only the firing of the missiles, which he said struck the target. Contrary to Soviet statements, there is no indication whatsoever that the interceptor pilot made any attempt either to communicate with the airliner or to signal it to land in accordance with accepted international practice.

She remarked: "Perhaps the most shocking fact learned from the transcript is that at no point did the pilots raise the question of the identity of the target aircraft, nor at any time did the interceptor pilot refer to it as anything other than 'the target.'" Reviewing the Soviet statements since the incident, Ambassador Kirkpatrick concluded: "None of these lies, half-lies and excuses can withstand examination. Straying off course is not recognized as a capital crime by civilized nations. No nation has the sovereign right to shoot down any person or vehicle that may stray across its border in peace time."

Once again the indictment went from the particular to the system that was responsible for the plane's destruction: some observers, she remarked, thought that this was not an isolated case of unconcern for human life but "a deliberate stroke designed to intimidate: a brutal, decisive act meant to instil fear and hesitation in all who observed its ruthless

violence, much as the destruction of an Afghan village or the imprison-
ment of the Helsinki monitors [by the Soviet authorities] are intended to
secure compliance through terror. Whichever the case . . . we are dealing
here not with pilot error, but with decisions and priorities characteristic
of a system." And she went on to quote Lenin in support of the proposition that "the Soviet Union is a state based on dual principles of callous-
ness and mendacity dedicated to the rule of force."[15]

The response by Soviet Ambassador Oleg Troyanovsky, clearly following his instructions, was little more than a lame rehearsal of the official
Soviet position. Meanwhile, however, Moscow had decided at last to acknowledge what could scarcely any longer be denied: the fact that a Soviet plane had downed the Korean jet. An official Soviet government
statement, which Troyanovsky read without apparent embarrassment to
the Security Council at its next session, the same afternoon, repeated the
previous account of Soviet warnings and attempts to communicate with
the intruder plane and continued:

> The regional Air Defense Forces command, having analyzed the
> actions of the intruder-plane and its route, which passed over military
> bases in the area of Sakhalin as well, finally came to the conclusion that
> a reconnaissance plane performing special missions was in USSR air-
> space. We also reached this conclusion because the plane's course was
> passing over strategically important regions of the Soviet Union. A
> fighter fired warning shots, using tracer shells, along the flight path of
> the intruder-plane. This measure is also provided for by international
> rules.
>
> Since even after this the intruder-plane did not obey the demand to
> head for a Soviet airfield and tried to escape, an air defense force fighter-
> interceptor fulfilled the command station's order to stop the flight. Such
> actions are fully in keeping with the Law on the USSR State Borders,
> which has been published.
>
> In stopping the intruder-plane's actions, the Soviet pilots could not
> know that it was a civilian airplane. It was flying without aerial naviga-
> tion lights, in the dead of night and in conditions of poor visibility, and
> it had not responded to signals.

The statement then made official the charges Soviet media had insistently
disseminated for days: the plane was sent over Soviet territory "to perform a spy mission." The plan, it alleged, was either to carry it out without hindrance or else "to turn all this into a large-scale political provocation directed against the Soviet Union."[16]

To complete our account of the Security Council deliberations: in
order to forge the broadest possible coalition prepared to vote for a
common resolution, the United States and Japan found themselves

obliged to remove a direct reference condemning the Soviet Union from the draft resolution introduced over this issue. After considerable haggling, the resolution came to a vote on September 12 and received nine favorable votes—the minimum needed for adoption—from Britain, France, Jordan, Malta, the Netherlands, Pakistan, Togo, the United States, and Zaire. Poland and the Soviet Union voted against it (the Soviet vote constituting a veto). Four other nations—China, Guyana, Nicaragua, and Zimbabwe—abstained.

As finally passed (and vetoed), the resolution, after reaffirming both the principles of territorial integrity and the necessity to adhere to internationally agreed procedures to deal with violations of airspace, stressing the need for an impartial investigation, expressing itself "gravely disturbed that a civil airliner of the Korean Air Lines on an international flight was shot down by Soviet military aircraft, with the loss of all 269 people on board," and reaffirming the right to appropriate compensation, proceeded to make an innocuous series of statements. It deplored the destruction of aircraft and lives; it declared such use of force incompatible with legal and humanitarian norms; it welcomed the forthcoming consideration of the incident by the International Civil Aviation Organization (ICAO); it invited the Secretary-General to conduct a speedy investigation; and it "decided to remain seized of the issue."[17] Thanks to the Soviet veto, the Security Concil failed to do so.

While Washington had decided to "hang tough"—at least in rhetoric—after the Soviet admission of responsibility,[18] Moscow provided further drama on September 9 by arranging an unprecedented two-hour press conference on live television with three senior officials, headed by Marshal Nikolai Ogarkov, chief of the Soviet General Staff, who made a detailed presentation of the official Soviet version of the events, and then, along with his two colleagues, answered questions, both friendly and hostile, from Soviet and foreign correspondents. He was flanked by First Deputy Foreign Minister Georgi Kornienko, in charge of American affairs, and Leonid Zamiatin, head of the International Information Department of the Communist Party Central Committee. The trio in this highly unusual performance, sponsored by the Defense and Foreign Ministries, was thus meant to represent Party, government, and the armed forces, with the marshal in the central ring.[19]

The impressive performance added relatively little new factual information. Ogarkov revealed that on the day of the incident the Soviet government had set up a special investigation commission, including experts from various departments (including the USSR State Committee for Civil

Aviation Safety), implying that the government statement of September 6 had awaited the commission's report. Ogarkov in turn claimed to be basing himself on its "facts and conclusions."

Once again he asserted that "it has been proved irrefutably that the intrusion of the South Korean airline's plane into Soviet airspace was a deliberate, carefully planned intelligence operation." He traced the plane's flight path: over Kamchatka "it was headed straight toward a major base of the USSR's strategic nuclear forces. It did not respond to any inquiries from Soviet air traffic control services and air defense planes." Over Sakhalin it allegedly changed direction, speed, and altitude, "obviously trying to evade the air defense planes," again passing over important military installations.

Since even after the warning shots were fired, Ogarkov continued, the plane "did not obey commands but tried to escape," a Soviet interceptor-plane "was given an order to stop its flight, and the order was carried out" by means of two air-launched missiles. "The termination of the flight," he declared, "was not an accident or an error," adding in reply to a question that the decision was made "by the regional command of the Air Defense Forces." Ogarkov added that thousands of foreign planes fly over Soviet territory and "nothing has happened to them" even in occasional cases of flight errors; "but in this case we are talking about something fundamentally different. . . . It was clear to all the command posts of the air defense system that they were dealing with a reconnaissance plane."

During the days following the press conference, Soviet media repeated many of its themes and provided variations on them—for instance, by publishing interviews with the pilot of the Soviet interceptor-plane which downed KAL 007 and with personnel at Soviet air defense ground stations in the Far East.[20] Presumably, the Soviet investigation of the incident continued; Marshal Ogarkov had referred to some of its findings, as had Ambassador Troyanovsky at the UN and as would the Soviet delegates at the ICAO meetings in Montreal in mid-September. Perhaps the most sophisticated (or at least complex) Soviet allegations came in an article by Air Marshal Piotr Kirsanov, arguing that the route and timing of the jetliner's flight were closely coordinated with three successive revolutions of a United States space reconnaissance satellite.[21] But the essentials of the Soviet version were now established and would remain unchanged.

In the United States, meanwhile, the State Department found itself obliged to issue some more corrections and additions to the translated transcript of the tape recording of the Soviet interceptors' messages to their ground control station: the new version, released on September 11, ostensibly the result of voice enhancement techniques and more careful listening, now included evidence that the Soviet fighter pilot had indeed reported having fired tracer (warning) shots at the jetliner prior to receiving the order to fire its missiles (as Moscow had claimed and Washington had heretofore denied).[22] But such details caused little more than minor embarrassment. The basic American version was and remained set.

The Administration could thus shift its attention increasingly to the political problems created by the jetliner episode at home. Continuing to argue with studied bluntness that the Soviet Union had "stonewalled the world" over its attack on the Korean aircraft, President Reagan concentrated on attempts to neutralize the charges coming from far-right critics in the United States that he had "caved in" and, whatever the rhetoric, remained "supine" in reacting to the Soviet "massacre." What would they have him do? he asked: vengeance was surely a poor guide to U.S. behavior. He used the occasion to remind his critics that (perhaps unlike Jimmy Carter) he had not been stunned by Soviet behavior: in fact, all the world could now see that he had been right when two years earlier he had said that the Soviets would lie, cheat, and do anything to promote world communism.[23]

The KAL 007 crisis had indeed unleashed a wave of popular revulsion, including demonstrations before Soviet consulates and embassies, the burning of Soviet flags and figures in effigy, and the boycott of Soviet goods and services, from vodka to airline flights, in a number of countries, from Japan to West Germany. While some of these were sponsored and exploited by extreme anti-Soviet groups, many were spontaneous and elicited intense feelings, by no means only from friends and relatives of the victims. A number of memorial services and protest rallies were held. A variety of planned Soviet visits and joint activities—be it a Soviet circus in Canada or a conference of Soviet and Western academics in the United States—were canceled or postponed. The aftermath of the incident led at least temporarily to a near-complete suspension of cultural and personal diplomacy.

And yet, by the end of the month, it appeared that passions were beginning to abate. On both sides, the amount of space in the press devoted to KAL 007 began to shrink, and new headlines and crises commanded readers' attention. Before long, civil aviation flights to and from the Soviet Union resumed. Negotiations over arms control continued—as it turned out, without producing agreement. But while Soviet-American relations returned to their customary level of vituperation and mutual suspicion, the unanswered questions and unresolved contradictions regarding the Korean jet loomed as large as ever.

The Flight Replayed

What, then, do we know about the flight of KAL 007 that seems beyond dispute? A regularly scheduled Korean Air Lines Boeing 747–230B, serial number 20559, left New York's John F. Kennedy International Airport on August 31 shortly after midnight (0405 GMT) on a direct and uneventful flight to Anchorage, Alaska, arriving there seven and one-half hours later. As is standard practice with KAL, new flight and cabin crews took over there; the aircraft was refueled and serviced for the remainder of the flight; a few passengers got off and others (airline personnel returning to South Korea) got on. Neither flight plan nor preflight operational data nor the various maintenance and service records from Anchorage suggest anything unusual; the captain, first officer, and flight engineer were all experienced, healthy, and familiar with the route.[24]

KAL 007 left Anchorage for Kimpo International Airport, Seoul, about 1300 GMT, some forty minutes behind official schedule. However, taking into account wind velocity, flight time was calculated to be seven hours and fifty-three minutes (instead of the scheduled eight hours and twenty minutes), which would have brought the jet into Seoul at approximately 6 A.M. Korean time (2100 GMT), prior to which customs and passenger handling were not available at Kimpo—a routine scheduling practice for Korean Air Lines.[25]

The flight plan called for the jet to proceed west from Anchorage to Bethel, Alaska, on standard ATS route J501, and from there to continue on a virtually straight line via ATS route R20. There are five international air traffic lanes between Alaska and Japan, of which the most northerly—i.e., the closest to Soviet territory—was R20 (or, as it is at times referred to, Red 20 or Romeo 20). This route was divided into some eight segments, separated by so-called VOR-established overwater checkpoints (VOR stands for "Very High Frequency Omni-bearing Range Radio Station"). Some of the checkpoints—identified by arbitrary names such as NABIE, NEEVA, NINNO, and NOKKA—are obligatory for planes to provide position reports; others are optional. (See Map 1.)

The plane reported to Anchorage ARTCC (Air Route Traffic Control Center) that it passed Bethel at 1349 hours and estimated passing over NABIE at 1430 hours. According to the subsequent ICAO investigation report, "radar data indicated that the aircraft started deviating from the assigned direct track to Bethel about ten minutes after departure and that the aircraft was about 6 NM [nautical miles] north of track when radar service [from Anchorage] was terminated [at 1327 hours]."[26] The radar recording at King Salmon, Alaska, which is not certified for civil air

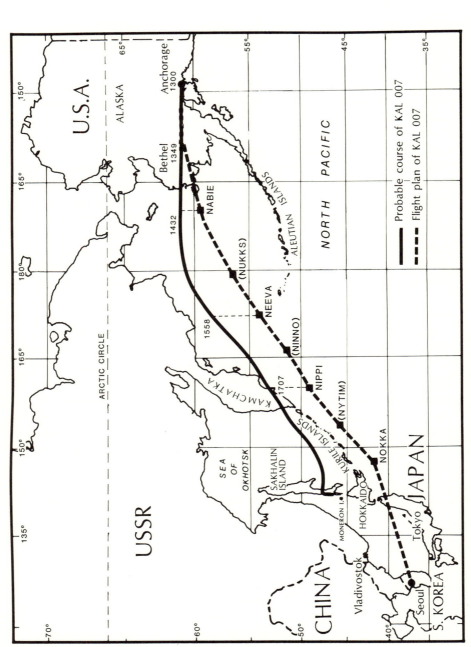

Map 1. Route of KAL 007, Route R20, and checkpoints

traffic control, showed the jet some twelve miles north of track when reporting to Bethel. The plane was thus flying a more northerly course than prescribed virtually from the start. Given the relatively minor deviation at the outset, Anchorage did not bother to inform the plane of it.

KAL 007 continued reporting as if on course: it checked in with NABIE at 1432 hours, estimating its passage over NEEVA, the next obligatory checkpoint, first at 1549 (as relayed to Anchorage by another Korean Air Lines jet, KAL 015, which had taken off behind KAL 007), than at 1553 (as provided directly by high-frequency radio from KAL 007 to Anchorage Radio). At 1558, it once again relayed a position report through KAL 015, ostensibly from NEEVA, estimating passing over NIPPI at 1708 hours. As requested, Anchorage ARTCC cleared KAL 007 to climb from 31,000 to 33,000 feet. Everything appeared in order.

The jet then established high-frequency radio contact with Tokyo Aeronautical Station. It reported passing over NIPPI at 1707, estimating that it would reach NOKKA (east of Hokkaido, where a change of direction would need to be made in the direction of Honshu) at 1826 hours. At 1815, the plane requested clearance to climb to 35,000 feet, which Tokyo provided at 1820. KAL 007 radioed Tokyo at 1823:05 hours that it had reached 35,000 feet.

As we now know, the plane was actually over Sakhalin Island, more than two hundred miles to the northwest, having flown a far more northerly route that had taken it over Kamchatka and the Sea of Okhotsk. There was nothing in its messages to Anchorage, Tokyo, or KAL 015 that would have led anyone to suspect that there was any problem with route or equipment. Three minutes after the jet had sent the last report to Tokyo, just cited, a Soviet air-defense fighter fired two rockets and reported at 1826:22, "The target is destroyed." At 1827:10, Tokyo received a message, presumably from KAL 007, which was unintelligible. This was the last signal received from the plane. All further efforts by Tokyo Radio to contact it were in vain. Subsequent work on the recording permitted Japanese acoustics research experts to decipher part of the message, transmitted in a high-pitched, frantic voice: it reported that the plane had "[lost] all engines, and rapid decompression."[27] (See Map 2.)

What had brought this catastrophe about? There are some uncertainties about the precise course KAL 007 had followed after passing north of Bethel (where Anchorage and King Salmon radar had last spotted it). But in any event, it had followed a course much closer to Soviet territorial waters than standard instructions, international agreements, and maps allowed. Soviet air defense forces (probably on Kamchatka Peninsula) which had followed the flight of the American RC-135 nearby began

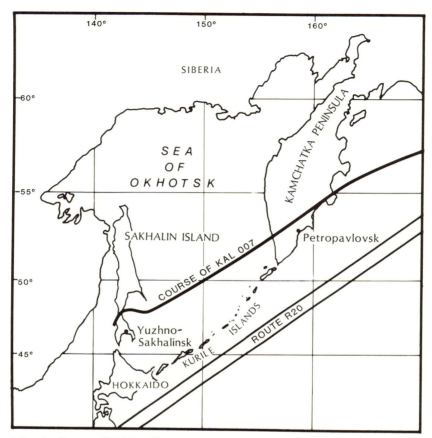

Map 2. Route of KAL 007, as presented by Marshal Ogarkov

tracking another plane in the same area and at about the same elevation, at 1551 hours. Moscow later asserted that, within ten minutes, the two radar blips—presumably for the RC-135 and KAL 007—"totally converged" and that for another ten minutes the two planes were on parallel course; whether or not this was an accurate reading will remain to be explored. Then, in the Soviet version, one of the planes turned back—an account which is compatible with the U.S. version, according to which the RC-135 returned to its base on Shemya Island, landing there at 1728 hours—about an hour before the Korean jet was downed. According to Marshal Ogarkov, by the time Soviet radar picked up the unidentified plane, at a point 800 kilometers (500 miles) northeast of Petropavlovsk-on-Kamchatka, it had already veered some 500 kilometers (300 miles) off its assigned track on R20.[28]

There are no grounds to question the official Soviet report stating that the "unidentified aircraft"—KAL 007—"violated the state frontier of the USSR" at 0530 Kamchatka time (1630 hours GMT), at an altitude of some 8,000 meters (about 26,250 feet), overflew the Kamchatka Peninsula from northeast to southwest, passing north of Petropavlovsk, and left it at 1708 (when the airliner was reporting that it was ostensibly over NIPPI, south of Kamchatka) at an altitude of 9,000 meters (about 29,500 feet).

In the Soviet version, the plane, once over Kamchatka, "was heading straight towards a major base of the USSR's strategic nuclear forces," ignoring various Soviet efforts to contact it by radio and to compel it to land at the nearest Soviet airfield.

The aircraft continued for more than an hour over international water—the Sea of Okhotsk—flying west of the Kurile Islands, unmolested but carefully observed. According to Marshal Ogarkov, the airliner, after having crossed the Sea of Okhotsk, at 1802 hours sharply changed direction as it again approached land, "circumventing the positions of our air defense missile units and passing over important military facilities in the southern part of Sakhalin Island." Now not only Soviet radar again detected the "unidentified plane"—this time, over Sakhalin—but the Japanese Air Defense Forces radar station at Wakkanai, at the northern tip of Hokkaido, at 1812 also spotted on their radar screens a previously unreported plane crossing Sakhalin, from northeast to southwest. At the time, it was alleged, the Japanese military personnel at the radar intelligence installation had no way of identifying this plane as KAL 007.[29]

The Soviet air defense command sent at least four interceptor planes—probably from Dolinsk-Sokol airbase on Sakhilin—after the unidentified "intruder." What follows is the transcript, translated from the Russian, of the transmissions from these four Soviet fighters over Sakhalin. Transmissions from the ground stations to the interceptors were not heard on the same tape. Pilots numbered 121, 731, and 805 are flying Soviet Su-15s (nicknamed Flagons); the one numbered 163 is flying a MiG-23 (nicknamed Flogger). The three ground stations are referred to by Soviet code names: *Deputat* (DEP), *Karnaval* (KAR), and *Trikotazh* (TRI). This is part of the transcript submitted by the United States to the UN Security Council, with corrections later introduced by the U.S. There is no reason to challenge the authenticity of the recording, presumably made by Japanese intelligence in the Wakkanai area as part of a routine effort of the United States and its allies to monitor Soviet electronic communications, and subsequently checked and translated by personnel of

the U.S National Security Agency. (According to Ambassador Kirkpatrick: "Nothing was cut from this tape. The recording was made on a
voice-activated recorder and, therefore, it covers only those periods of
time when conversation was heard.")[30]

Time	To	From	Message
1800:46	DEP	121	Course 100 [refers to directional heading with magnetic north at 0 degrees, magnetic south at 180] in a climb to 8,000 meters [26,250 ft.]. I don't understand. What course? . . . My course is 100.
1800:57	DEP	121	Am executing.
1802:11	DEP	121	Course 50.
1805:14	KAR	163	I am answering.
1805:53	DEP	805	805 is on course 240.
1805:56	DEP	805	I am watching.
1806:00	DEP	805	Roger. Understood. I'm flying behind.
1806:07	KAR	163	Course 30, 8,000 meters.
1806:22	KAR	163	Executing course 100.
1806:30	DEP	805	Roger. . . . Distance to airfield?
1806:33	DEP	805	Roger.
1806:45	KAR	163	[Altitude] 4,900. . . . Am executing.
	DEP	121	Don't understand.
1807:04	KAR	163	Am executing.
1807:50	DEP	805	Fuel remainder three [metric] tons.
	DEP	805	Roger. Repeat the course.
	DEP	805	To the left, probably? Not to the right.
1808:06	DEP	805	Carry out course 260.
	DEP	805	On course 260. . . . Understood.
	KAR	163	Course 220. 7,500 meters [about 24,600 ft.].
	DEP	805	Roger.
1808:31	DEP	805	Should I turn off the weapons system? . . . Roger.
1808:48	KAR	163	163 needs to drop his wing tanks.
1809:00	DEP	805	Yes, it [KAL 007] has turned. . . . The target is 80 degrees to my left.
1809:35	DEP	805	Executing [course] 240.
1809:44	DEP	805	Course 240. . . . Roger.
1810:16	DEP	805	Executing [course] 220.
1810:25	DEP	121	Executing.
1810:29	KAR	163	[Course] 245 for 163? . . . Executing.
1810:35	DEP	805	Course 220.
1810:44	DEP	805	I don't understand.
1810:51	DEP	805	Roger. The [anti-collision?] light is blinking.

1810:57	KAR	163	Course 245. 7,500 meters.
1811:20	DEP	805	8,000 meters.... Roger.
1811:28	DEP	121	Course 280.
1811:37	DEP	163	4,500 meters [about 14,750 ft.].
	DEP	121	Course 280.
1811:51	DEP	805	Executing.
1812:03	KAR	163	Executing.
1812:10	DEP	805	I see it visually and on [radar] screen.
1812:15	DEP	805	Roger.
1812:21	KAR	163	Executing 10 left.
1812:41	KAR	163	I have dropped my tanks.... Dropped them.... Executing.
1813:05	DEP	805	I am watching it. I'm locked on to the target.
1813:16	DEP	805	Roger.
1813:26	DEP	805	The target isn't responding to inquiry [IFF= Identification/Friend or Foe].
1813:35	DEP	805	The target's course is 240 degrees.
1813:40	DEP	805	[The weapons system] is turned on.
1814:10	DEP	805	Roger. Still on the same course for now.
1814:16	DEP	805	Roger.
1814:34	DEP	805	Roger. I have [enough] speed. I don't need to turn on my afterburner.
1814:41	DEP	805	My fuel remainder is 2,700.
	KAR	163	I've dropped my tanks. One at 4,000. One at 3,800.
1815:00	KAR	163	My course is 230.
1815:08	DEP	805	The target's course is still the same, 240.
1815:37	KAR	163	Executing.
1815:47	DEP	805	I am in lock-on.
1815:51	DEP	805	Course is 240.
1816:46	DEP	805	The target's course is 240.
	KAR	163	Yes.
1817:05	KAR	163	Repeat the azimuth.
1817:10	DEP	163	1001 [Take control of me] from KARNAVAL. Azimuth 45. Distance 60.
	DEP	163	Roger.
1817:24	KAR	163	DEPUTAT watches me [on radar].
1817:34	KAR	163	DEPUTAT is inquiring: Do you see the target or not?
1817:41	KAR	163	Do you see?
1817:49		805	Are you calling 805?
1817:58		805	Who's calling 805?
1818:03	DEP	805	I see it!
1818:09	DEP	163	KARNAVAL does not see.

1818:12	DEP	805	Repeat.
1818:19	DEP	805	Executing.
1818:34	DEP	805	The ANO [air navigation lights] are burning. The light is flashing.
1818:56	DEP	163	Roger. I'm at 7,500. Course 230.
1819:02	DEP	805	I am closing on the target.
1819:08	DEP	805	They do not see me.
1819:20	DEP	121	Executing.
1819:44	DEP	163	I am flying behind the target at a distance of 25 [kilometers]. Do you see [me]?
1819:55	DEP	163	[Call]
1820:08	DEP	805	Fiddlesticks, I'm on. That is, my Z.G. [indicator] is lit [missile warhead is locked on]. (upset)
1820:12	DEP	805	Answering.
1820:17	DEP	805	I answered.
1820:22	DEP	805	[I] need to approach it [closer].
1820:30	DEP	805	I'm turning lock-on off and I'm approaching the target.
1820:41	DEP	163	[For] 163?
1820:49	DEP	805	I have broken off lock-on. I am firing cannon bursts. [According to Ogarkov, four bursts of warning shots with a total of 120 tracer shells were fired.]
	DEP	163	[Right now I can't?] see it.
	DEP	805	Exactly. I have executed.
1821:17	DEP	163	Executing.
1821:24	DEP	805	Yes. I am approaching the target. I am going in closer.
1821:35	DEP	805	The target's light is blinking. I have already approached the target to a distance of about 2 kilometers [1.2 miles].
1821:40	DEP	805	The target [elevation] is at 10,000 meters [32,800 ft.].
1821:51	DEP	163	I see both [target and 805]. Distance 10, 15 kilometers.
1821:55	DEP	805	What are instructions?
1821:59	DEP	163	Roger.
1822:02	DEP	805	The target is decreasing speed.
1822:17	DEP	805	I am going around it. I'm already moving in front of the target.
1822:23	DEP	805	I have increased speed.
1822:29	DEP	805	No. [It is] decreasing speed.
1822:42	DEP	805	It should have been [done] earlier. How can I chase it? I am already abeam of the target. (upset)
1822:55	DEP	805	Now I have to fall back a bit from the target.
1823:05	DEP	805	Repeat.
1823:10	DEP	805	The target's altitude is 10,000 meters.
1823:18	DEP	805	From me it is located 70 degrees to the left.
1823:37	DEP	805	I'm dropping back already. Now I will try the rockets.

1823:49 DEP 163 12 [kilometers] to the target. I see both.
        DEP 121 I am in a right turn on a course of 300.

[According to Soviet sources, at 1824 the ground station—presumably *Deputat*—ordered the Su-15, i.e., 805, to "stop" (*presech'*, literally arrest or interdict) the flight of the intruder, as the planes were nearing the small town of Pravda on the southwest coast of Sakhalin.]

1824:15 DEP 121 Executing.
1824:22 DEP 805 Roger. I am in lock-on.
1824:56 DEP 121 I am turning to a course of 30.
              121 Roger.
1825:11 DEP 805 I am closing on the target, am in lock-on. Distance to the target is 8 kilometers [5 miles].
1825:16 DEP 805 I have already switched it on.
1825:33 DEP 121 On a course of 30.
1825:46 DEP 805 Z.G. [missile warheads locked on].
1826:20 DEP 805 I have executed the launch.
1826:22 DEP 805 The target is destroyed.
1826:27 DEP 805 I am breaking off attack.[31]

On orders from his ground command, Su-15 pilot 805 had fired two air-to-air AA-3 Anab missiles, of which at least one and probably both hit the jet within seconds. While Japanese and Soviet monitoring of the plane's fate at that moment was imperfect, apparently the jet remained on the radar screens for another twelve minutes, until 1838 hours GMT. At 1830 hours, radar showed 007 at 16,000 feet. Seeking later to reconstruct the plane's final minutes, Japanese Defense Agency officials found it likely that, after being struck by the Soviet missile (or missiles), the severely crippled KAL 007 descended in "vast spirals" down to about 2,000 feet elevation and then, having left Soviet territory, plunged vertically into the sea.[32]

There were no survivors. The extensive and bitterly contested multinational search for bodies, debris, and the "black boxes" from the plane yielded little of help or value: some unidentifiable human remains, hundreds of pieces of metal and equipment, a few personal articles, but no trace of the flight data and cockpit voice recorders, or so both the Soviet and the American-Japanese teams involved reported. After more than two months, the search and rescue operations were closed down.[33]

2

How and Why: Explications and Explanations I

The story of KAL 007, as we have tried to relate it, raises more questions than there are satisfactory answers. It is instructive that a limited set of events, occurring virtually—but not quite—in front of our eyes, reported in the daily papers and on television screens, can be so mystifying to the observer. That there are doubts about motives and intentions should not be surprising: that, after all, is true in all human affairs. That there should also be such fundamental uncertainty concerning the events themselves and their causes may be more disconcerting, especially when it applies not only to the Soviet Union but also to the United States and its friends.

Research and reflection cannot entirely remove the vast areas of conflicting allegations, nor can they fill the substantial gaps in evidence; but a careful review of the available information and a more or less systematic exploration of alternative hypotheses and explanations can help shrink the parameters of uncertainty. This is what this chapter and the next set out to do. It will be useful to organize them around two distinct questions: first, what explains the behavior of KAL 007? and second, what explains Soviet behavior in the crisis? While the two questions are of course related—if only by the central event of the crisis itself—the answer to one does not depend on the answer to the other; nor need our uncertainty about the answer to either contaminate our convictions about the other question.

Why Did KAL 007 Stray?

The South Korean airliner en route from Anchorage to Seoul flew over Kamchatka, the Sea of Okhotsk, and Sakhalin Island before being shot down. At its greatest deviation from the flight plan, it was over 300 miles' off course. The plane had sophisticated modern equipment and an experienced crew. There are only four categories of reasons that might account for its deviation from the normal track which had been prescribed by its computerized flight plan:

1. Causes beyond the control of the plane's flight crew; mechanical failure of navigation equipment and hijacking are obvious candidates in this group.

2. Innocent human error, unintended and presumably undetected;* or incapacitation of the crew during the flight.

3. Wilful action by the captain, co-pilot, and flight engineer, for essentially nonpolitical reasons; saving time or fuel by flying the most direct route would fall into this rubric; so would sheer adventurism.

4. Deliberate action by at least some of the crew in fulfillment of a surreptitious assignment or mission, such as carrying out a secret task for a South Korean or American intelligence agency.

These are logically exhausting alternatives: the cause was either beyond the crew's control or it was not; the deviation was either intended or unintended; it was either known to the crew or it was not; it either constituted a secret mission or it did not.

The Innocent Versions

What about causes outside the control of the flight crew? There were, especially during the early weeks of the crisis, occasional suggestions from Korean Air Lines officials that the jet's deflection from its proper course must have been due to the use of a portable computer by a passenger on board. While personal computers can cause electronic confusion on airplanes, there are no known cases of unintended deflection comparable to the KAL 007 episode and no solid technical grounds to make such an hypothesis credible.[1] Or else, KAL president Cho Choong Hoon suggested, the most likely reason why the airliner lost its direction was intentional Soviet jamming: "The possibility is high that the Soviet Union has developed a system to cause planes to lose their direction."[2] In fact, such an hypothesis must be dismissed as fanciful and at best farfetched. Similarly, hypotheses that unusual winds or magnetic variation had somehow caused the plane to lose its bearings—for the entire duration of the flight, and

---

* It is of course possible to imagine a scenario in which innocent error was detected by the cockpit crew during the final minutes of the flight, as the Soviet interceptors came near. This might account for the "evasive" action allegedly taken over Sakhalin, according to Soviet accounts, and would support one hypothesis according to which the aircraft had no lights on over Kamchatka but did have them on over Sakhalin. However, this would not be consistent with the innocuous (and incorrect) position reports broadcast by KAL 007 until the end.

undetected by any flight personnel—appear devoid of any serious basis.[3]

Finally, persons close to the John Birch Society speculated in the days following the crash that the plane had been hijacked by Soviet agents wishing to dispose of the society's president, Congressman Larry Mc-Donald, who was a passenger on the plane. There are obvious difficulties with this scenario: for instance, the captain did not activate the hidden hijacking alert system on the plane; there were apparently nonuniformed sky marshals aboard, as is customary on international KAL flights; if this had been a pro-Soviet hijacking, the Soviet fighters' attack would have made no sense; and, of course, considering the panoply of possible enemies—and victims—of the Soviet Union worldwide, it is hard to believe that Moscow would choose Congressman McDonald for such unique and costly victimization (even assuming that it would have known of his travel plans sufficiently in advance to get its own agents aboard).[4] The hijacking option can safely be put to rest.

More serious are the hypotheses of equipment malfunction or innocent error in its use. The aircraft was equipped with three inertial navigation systems (INS), three VHF (very high frequency) and two HF (high frequency) radio transceivers, two transponders, two weather radars, four receivers, and a variety of other altimeters, indicators, compass systems, autothrottles and autopilots.[5] Of these the prime candidates for malfunction were the INS systems.

The Boeing 747 had three redundant Litton LTN-72R INS systems, any one of which can, when connected to the plane's autopilot system, steer it to a succession of nine positions or checkpoints en route to a destination. A light signal indicates each change of direction, speed, or altitude at the designated checkpoints. While the INS—initially developed for guidance of ballistic missiles—requires technologically sophisticated equipment to operate, the performance record of the INS has been excellent, and aviation industry professionals as well as civil aviation administrators rather unanimously dismiss as exceedingly small the likelihood of simultaneous mechanical failure or malfunction of all three independent INS, which had previously worked without noticeable error.

Even more unlikely is the scenario in which their total failure remained entirely undiscovered by the plane's flight crew: the malfunction hypothesis assumes an alert crew not engaged in any secret mission. In fact, the plane's personnel never in their various transmissions after leaving Anchorage indicated the slightest suspicion of equipment malfunction or their awareness of flying the wrong route. Moreover, during the flight the crew provided position reports to ground control, including expected time of arrival at the next way point, wind velocity, and other pertinent information presumably supplied by well-functioning INS equipment.

Assuming the very unlikely combination of circumstances by which all three INS had suddenly malfunctioned and that for some reason the flight crew during the entire flight had had no inkling that anything was wrong, the crew still had available to it the weather radar system, which in its ground mapping mode would have shown clearly when KAL 007 was flying over or near land—such as Kamchatka and Sakhalin—at a time when the flight plan (and the flight crew's position reports to Anchorage and Narita) had it over water. (If, on the other hand, the radar system was in the weather mode over Sakhalin, it should have picked up the Soviet interceptors nearby.) The plane was equipped with two Bendix RDR-IF weather radar sets, which had a range of 200 nautical miles with a 180 degree scan capability.[6] There is no reason to suspect that the radar system was not functioning properly, and normal procedures called for its use in the ground mapping mode.

Finally, while there is some question about the radio contact by KAL 007 during the flight (at times relayed through another Korean airliner, not an unusual occurrence on this route), its multiple VHF and HF radio systems permitted it at all times to be in touch with either a U.S. or a Japanese air traffic control center. Not until the garbled message sent after the Su-15's missiles had hit the plane did any radio communication from KAL 007 suggest any mishap or any awareness of being off course. All in all, the hypothesis of equipment failure—while it cannot be entirely disproven—deserves to be relegated to the category of least likely events.

This leaves the possibility of inadvertent, innocent human error—a set of surmises which by their very nature are difficult to test, prove, or disprove. That such errors occur, however infrequently, seems well established. A study based on reports compiled by the U.S. National Aeronautics and Space Administration (NASA) lists a total of twenty-one cases over five years in which U.S. airline pilots found themselves off course—in most of these twenty-one instances, as a result of trifling errors, such as the transposition of two digits in entering coordinates into the INS computer. True, this is an insignificant number if we consider that these are twenty-one instances in something like two million flights (or approximately 0.00001 percent), or that only about one flight in ten thousand strays fifty or more miles off course.[7] On the other hand, the low statistical incidence of such occurrences tells us nothing about the one particular case we are interested in, which is not determined by the law of averages. If we relied on probabilities, the unlikely would never be expected to occur.

In the absence of any specific leads or information, the best that can be done is to establish, by calculation or by simulation, what errors *could* have produced the known result—that is, the particular route flown by KAL 007 on the fateful night—and to speculate whether such errors and their consequences could have remained undetected by the crew during the entire flight.

On the technical side, we are greatly aided here by the investigation conducted by the International Civil Aviation Organization, which included four simulation flights testing particular errors in programming or use of the INS; others have attempted less rigorous simulations. While numerous variations have been proposed, three major possibilities have been suggested to explain the jet's course.

A first surmise concerns the entries into the INS computer. If, instead of being routed over the various checkpoints on R20, between Alaska and Hokkaido, the plane was accidentally programmed to fly directly to Seoul by the shortest route, the result (it was proposed) might have been something like the route taken by KAL 007. This might have been the result of using one of the three INS computers which is normally limited to such tasks as checking distances and time, to set the aircraft's course. If the flight crew was watching the other two computers which were correctly programed, it might fail to detect the problem. The ICAO study showed, however, that this scenario would have been difficult to reconcile with the position reports received from the aircraft. Moreover, the most direct route to Seoul—the so-called Great Circle route—would have taken the plane across Kamchatka and Sakhalin much to the north of the line which according to Soviet and Japanese radar it actually took.[8] This explanation—not as a cover-up but as the real cause of the intrusion into Soviet airspace—would therefore seem to create more problems than it resolves.

The second variant hypothesizes that on the plane's instrument panel in the cockpit a five-position switch which sets the mode of operation of the automatic pilot was inadvertently left in the wrong position: instead of being set on INS, it may have been turned to "heading mode," which would have kept the aircraft on a steady course, subject to change by the pilot; the other three positions are ILS (instrument landing system), LAND (automatic landing), and VOR/LOC (locked on to a particular radio beacon). If a magnetic heading of, say, 246 degrees was chosen, and if we allow for winds, this would have taken KAL 007 well north of its flight plan into the vicinity of the route which it appears to have traveled, at about the right time.[9] (See Map 3.)

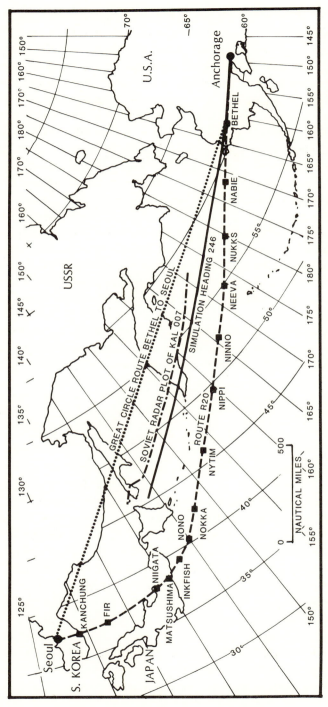

Map 3. Simulation of 246-degree heading, Great Circle route, and Soviet radar plot of KAL 007 (based on *ICAO Report*)

A third hypothesis deals with the simple numerical transposition of digits in entering the coordinates in one or more of the INS computers. The most plausible variant posits a scenario in which, when inserting the coordinates for the plane's position, a ten degree error in longitude was made for Anchorage (W139° instead of W149°). This would have started the plane on a course of ostensibly over 600 miles to Bethel, instead of the actual 300, and would therefore have taken it a good deal to the west and north of the start of R20. A simulation of this alternative revealed that, while the aircraft could in this fashion have followed its actual track, neither distances nor times between (real or assumed) checkpoints on R20 could have been mistakenly taken to conform to KAL 007's flight plan; for instance, when reporting from "actual" Bethel, the INS would have shown it to be 296 miles away. But a variant set of assumptions— feeding the wrong coordinates into only one of the three INS computers and not activating the automatic cross-check among them—permitted developing a simulation in which the actual track of KAL 007 was realistically replicated, while the flight crew might have been misled by the computer read-out.[10]

Such a sequence of events cannot be ruled out. True, the follow-up reports from the ICAO's own Air Navigation Commission, a few months later, concluded (without elaborating further):

> The Commission found it difficult to validate and endorse the conclusions connected with the scenarios postulated in the Secretary General's report because any [*sic*] of them contained some points which could not be explained satisfactorily.[11]

Moreover, when it came to entering the needed data in the INS computer—in this instance, in Anchorage—"the KAL procedures required each flight crew member to check the present (ramp) position entry."[12] Normal procedure called for one of the senior officers—pilot, copilot, or flight engineer—to put the data on the screen by means of the computer keyboard and for one of the others to check it before it was entered into the INS. It also required the data to be entered separately for each of the three INS computers rather than mechanically copying it from one to the other two. In practice, of course, such procedures become a matter of routine, especially for experienced flight personnel, and shortcuts are commonly used. A number of aviation personnel have dropped hints (without wishing to be quoted on the subject) that Korean Air Lines personnel had the reputation for occasionally "macho," cavalier, or sloppy performance and for cutting corners. Even if true, such a reputation tells us nothing about the flight crew's behavior on this particular flight. (See Plate 1 and Map 4.)

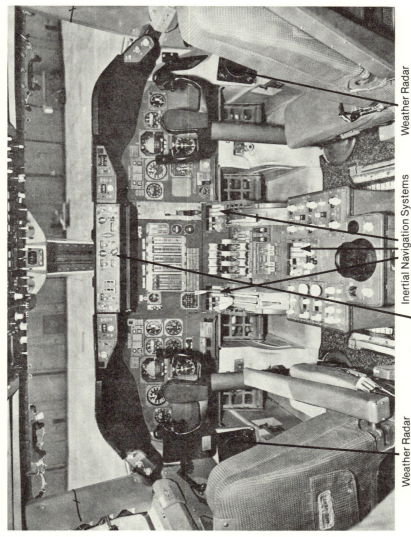

Weather Radar

Inertial Navigation Systems

Automatic Pilot Switch/
Navigation Mode Selector

Weather Radar

NOTE: Neither Korean Airlines nor Boeing will, for legal reasons, release a photograph of the actual configuration of the cockpit in the plane used for the fatal flight of KAL 007. Since the particular airliner used on that occasion had been purchased second-hand by KAL from Lufthansa, it is likely to have had a slightly different configuration of the instrumentation than that shown here.

Plate 1. Cockpit of the Boeing 747 (Courtesy of Boeing Commercial Airline Company)

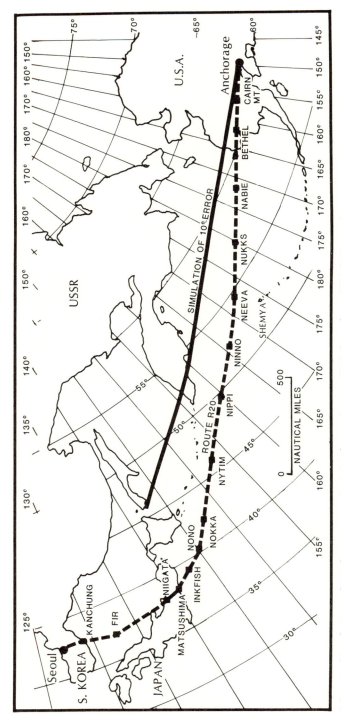

Map 4. Simulation of 10-degree error in initial position on INS (based on *ICAO Report*)

What we know about the flight crew is the following. The pilot in command, Captain Chun Byung In, 45 years old, had joined KAL in 1972 after ten years' service in the South Korean air force. He was considered a superior pilot and had in fact been selected to fly the aircraft used by President Chun of the Republic of Korea on a tour of Southeast Asia in 1981. His total flight experience exceeded 10,000 hours, including over 6,500 hours on a B747. In 1982, he had received a citation for his accident-free record, and he had flown route R20 at least twenty-seven times, most recently on August 16.

The co-pilot, First Officer Son Dong Hwi, 47 years old, had served nineteen years in the Korean air force before joining KAL in 1979. His flight experience came close to 9,000 hours, including thirty flights on route R20, most recently on August 14.

The flight engineer, Kim Eui Dong, born in 1951, had served in the Korean Marine Aviation Corps for four years before joining KAL in 1977. While this was his first flight on route R20, he had completed all the requisite courses for the B707 and B747 and had amassed over 4,000 hours experience as flight engineer.

There is nothing to suggest that the flight crew was in less than first-rate condition at the time of the fatal flight.[13]

There are, then, at least two scenarios which, at a minimum, are not implausible, can be more or less reconciled with the known facts, and conform to the record of at least occasional, if rare, actual occurrences. Despite the reservations voiced concerning them, their technical possibility is supported by the simulations and calculations undertaken by the ICAO investigation team in conjunction with Korean and United States aviation authorities, Litton Aero Products, and the Boeing Aircraft Company (which conducted the simulations).[14]

What is required to accept either of these versions at face value is the assumption that during the entire flight—some five and one-half hours— none of the experienced and skilled crew (nor anyone else aboard) found anything amiss, and during the repeated instrument checks required for reporting by radio when passing over the various way points (reports which we know were made)[15] never discovered that KAL 007 was dramatically off course. And this in spite of the fact that all flight crews flying R20 were of course keenly aware—and repeatedly reminded in manuals and on maps—that this was the North Pacific route closest to Soviet territory (typically, at a distance of about fifty miles but at certain points a good deal closer), that flying through Soviet airspace was both forbidden and dangerous,[16] and that violations of standing rules in this regard courted severe penalties.

Moreover, the number of possible and likely cross-checks—both automatic and manual—was simply too great to let the hypothesis of inadvertent error (such as leaving the INS switch, by mistake, on the heading mode) stand without serious question. Henry Duffy, of the Air Line Pilots Association, remarked, after reviewing the various backup systems: "Every time we come up with a theory, we find maybe two cross-checks that should have told him [the KAL 007 pilot] he was wrong." And Canadian general Richard Rohmer concludes in regard to this explanation: "Impossible to believe."[17]

The same hypothesis also requires accepting as believable the assertion that during the Soviet attempts to intercept the aircraft, all flight personnel on KAL 007 were utterly oblivious to the proximity of Soviet interceptors or to their activities. Whether or not we credit Soviet claims that they attempted to contact the plane by radio and that the Soviet fighter made the visual maneuvers internationally agreed upon for such interceptions, we do know that it finally fired tracer shells along the path of KAL 007's flight. At the time all this was taking place right around the plane, its flight crew was in radio communication with ground control stations but never betrayed the slightest suggestion of anything unusual taking place.[18] Even the very bland ICAO report concludes that "each of the scenarios assumes a considerable degree of lack of alertness and attentiveness on the part of the entire flight crew but not to a degree that is unknown in international civil aviation."[19] It might be more accurate to reverse the proposition by suggesting that, while one cannot assert that such irresponsible carelessness and failure to follow regulations could not have occurred, on a commercial flight by a competitive airline, with some 240 passengers aboard, it does require a substantial act of imagination to accept this as the best explanation for what took place.

We are thus left with two incompatible versions to pursue. According to one, the plane was totally oblivious to what was going on. This would be consistent with its position reports and radio messages throughout. As the ICAO report stated: "No evidence was found during the [ICAO] investigation that the flight crew of KE007* was, at any time, aware of the flight's deviation from its planned route in spite of the fact that it continued along the same general off-track flight path for some five hours and 26 minutes."[20] Indeed, a great number of details, such as the plane's failure to evade the pursuit of Soviet interceptors or to respond to their warnings, and even the jet's final radio message, would seem to support such oblivion.

---

*KE007 is the abbreviated notation for Korean Air Lines flight 007 used in the international civil aviation and Air Traffic Control systems.

Or else we must hold, with Richard Rohmer, that "the answer to the question, 'Did the 747's crew know the aircraft was off course?' is 'Yes, they knew exactly where they were from the time they left Anchorage through the false way point checks that they transmitted past Kamchatka and over Sakhalin Island to their destruction.'"[21] Both versions are possible. The second, to be credible, requires us to believe in the deliberate diversion of the aircraft from its flight plan. If it was done for essentially nonpolitical and relatively innocuous—if in this instance fatal—reasons, such a scenario must assume the collusion of at least a few key members of the flight crew, such as the pilot, co-pilot, and flight engineer, for they would need to agree on the instrument settings, the direction heading, and the need to provide ground traffic control stations with fictitious reports on location and perhaps on temperature and winds.

In substance, the purpose of such a maneuver would have been to take a shortcut from Anchorage to Seoul—perhaps something close to the so-called Great Circle Route—which would have saved some distance (178 NM), time (twenty minutes), and fuel (perhaps 7,000 pounds). The total hypothetical saving has been estimated at some $2,500. In fact, KAL 007 was not even close to this route and thus would have saved a good deal less. Why should this have been a compelling motive for Captain Chun and his crew?

It has been suggested that taking the more direct route would have obviated the need for a refueling stop in Japan; but in fact the 747 had a very full tank, well in excess of what was needed to reach Seoul (263,700 pounds on departure from Anchorage, with an estimated burn-off of 206,400 during the flight), and no refueling stop was ever contemplated. As was standard, fuel calculations included a reserve for diversion to an alternate airport (Kimhae, forty extra minutes), for holding (thirty extra minutes), and for other contingencies (an extra 10 percent).[22] A well-informed analysis suggested soon after the flight:

> The motive for this action could have been economic. The Great Circle route between NEEVA and Seoul is shorter than the Romeo 20 route and in normal circumstances would provide a valuable saving in fuel, but no pilot would fly over most of the Soviet Union's conventional and nuclear military installations in East Asia in order to save a sum of about US $2,500.[23]

Nor is it clear who would have benefited from the fuel saving: while there has been inevitable speculation concerning some kickback to the flight crew, there is, as we shall see, scant indication that it would have earned anything but a word of admonition or perhaps thanks.

There is, however, a more elaborate (but scarcely any more convincing) hypothesis on behalf of this version. It centers on the financial condition and the business ethos of Korean Air Lines. KAL's management has in fact not been particularly forthcoming about its affairs, but this scarcely suffices to make it suspect.

Rohmer, who is the prime advocate of this version, stresses KAL's rapid growth, aggressive management, and heavy debts—in excess of a billion dollars in 1982. But if in 1980–81 KAL had posted losses, so had other airlines, and in 1982 it showed a modest profit. According to this version, the severe cost-cutting by KAL included an effort by its loyal personnel to shave a little time off its flights and thus help the company balance its books. But this meant that KAL flights would routinely arrive at their destinations ahead of scheduled arrival time. This has simply not been the case. On many routes there is no way of "cutting corners." No other instances of such alleged cost-cutting have come to light (other than KAL pilots pushing out of turn ahead of other planes stacked up over an airport). If it were a common practice, many KAL employees, present and former, would be aware of it, and one might have expected at least one to come forward to testify to it, especially since to the strongly anti-Soviet South Korean fliers this would help clear the United States of the suspicion of having used the KAL 007 for an intelligence operation.

Moreover, not only is there no record of any previous deviations from KAL 007's flight plan; Japanese radar operators would be well aware of it if this were a common practice.[24] French sources, who do not wish to be identified, have reported an unconfirmed story according to which KAL management routinely returned to the crew something like 60 percent of the cash equivalent of the saving effected.[25] If so, not only would this have vastly enlarged the pool of potential "co-conspirators," it would also greatly reduce the resulting saving. If, hypothetically, KAL 007 had saved three-fifths of the amount saved by flying the Great Circle route, the $1,500 would have been divided so that 60 percent, or $900, went to the crew (how many members of it?) and $600 to the company. It defies all good sense to take seriously the notion that, presumably with connivance of company officials, the flight courted death and destruction for $600.

Dismissing this explanation, one might still speculate that the flight crew decided to take the shorter route simply on a dare or out of a sense of adventure. Observers have, for instance, suggested a scenario in which the pilot—a proud and much decorated officer—might have bragged to other crew members about having flown through Soviet airspace with impunity on other occasions, and then found himself challenged to repeat such a feat. Or else the flight crew of KAL 007 might have been engaged in a race with KAL 015, which was also proceeding from Anchorage to Seoul some fifteen minutes behind it but staying on its assigned track; this version has gained some piquancy from the fact that the pilot of KAL 015, which during the flight had transmitted several messages from 007 to Anchorage, later resigned from the airline and declined to testify in one of the civil suits brought against it.

Leaving aside the fact that there is nothing in the personnel's record to suggest such irresponsibility, there has also been no evidence that such maneuvers were ever attempted—or carried out—on this route on other occasions; we are told that there is no record of deviations of more than ten miles from the R20 track. True, one British comment asserts that "airliners flying this route often fly around Kamchatka, then through the LaPérouse Strait [separating Hokkaido from Sakhalin], to save time and fuel, instead of taking the authorised but longer way south of Hokkaido."[26] But even if true, this does not refer to Korean Air Lines, and it implies careful avoidance of Soviet airspace. Just like the earlier quotation, it assumes that the flight proceeded on R20 past Kamchatka and only then, perhaps at NEEVA, turned to a direct track to Seoul. In fact, we know that this was not the case on the night of August 31/ September 1. Still, even the official ICAO report remarks that "it was alleged by some sources that pilots of Korean Air Lines have in the past made a practice of taking short cuts when operating on the North Pacific routes." It hastens to add: "Such short cuts were not possible without either flying through FIRs [flight information regions] of the USSR where such flights would be observed or without later being observed by civil and/or self-defense force radars in Japan. There were no records of such deviations." It adds:

> If KE007 had deliberately overflown Soviet territory without authorization, while making position reports along the assigned route, it would have been reasonable to assume that the pilot would have familiarized himself with the regulations concerning flight over USSR territory and the rules concerning danger and prohibited areas promulgated in the Aeronautical Information Publication (AIP) USSR.[27]

The pilot's or the flight crew's behavior would have been essentially the same, whatever the possible motive, if a deliberate effort was made to take the jet to Seoul by a shortcut.

A related speculation deserves mention, if only to be dismissed: the possibility that it was the frequent practice of KAL pilots to proceed home through Soviet airspace, generally undetected and undisturbed, as part of their general style of cutting corners. There is nothing to support this hypothesis, which requires more South Korean trust in Soviet benevolence and perhaps also a greater belief in Soviet incompetence than the facts appear to warrant. This does not deny the possibility that such attempts may have been made on earlier occasions, for which there is no documentary support.

Technically it would have been easy to take a shortcut: all it would have taken was to punch in the coordinates of Seoul for a straight flight there, without the intervening checkpoints on R20. As we have seen, there are several serious objections to this hypothesis. It would have required the plane to misreport all its positions. The Great Circle route (say, from Bethel, Alaska, to Seoul) would have taken the aircraft considerably deeper into Soviet territory than it in fact went. And if for some reason the plane were to fly through Soviet airspace, it remains unclear what incentives could have led a rational, well-informed pilot and his colleagues to embark on a flight which was virtually certain to be detected and thus, in the view of other pilots, was tantamount to suicide.[28]

To be sure, one cannot peremptorily discount the possibility of such a decision—deliberate or impulsive—to proceed to Seoul by way of Soviet airspace. If so, the crew would of course have sought to conceal it from ground traffic controllers. But this explanation for the jet's deviation from the assigned route also requires a number of other assumptions that make this an unlikely—though not an impossible—solution to the puzzle before us. One of the most compelling considerations here is the fact that, having successfully crossed Kamchatka, the aircraft could have considered its derring-do (or fuel-saving) achieved and continued outside of Soviet airspace without overflying Sakhalin Island, either by going south of Sakhalin over the Sea of Japan, or by aiming at Hokkaido, essentially back to what had been the prescribed flight plan. But it must be recognized that the same argument—the "unnecessary" overflight of Sakhalin after Kamchatka had been crossed—may also be used to support the view that the aircraft's crew was utterly unaware of where it was in fact flying. That is, the argument about avoiding Sakhalin does not make sense (1) if either the crew was not aware of where it was, or (2) if flying over Sakhalin was part of its plan.[29]

Mysterious Mission?

We are thus left with the fourth possible scenario: a mission undertaken by some of the members of the flight crew of KAL 007, presumably on behalf of an American (and/or South Korean) government agency.*

It should be stated emphatically that there is no solid or conclusive evidence in support of this hypothesis—no more than there was for any of the earlier three we have sketched above. By the same token, this one deserves to be weighed and considered as seriously as were the other three.

The fact that this is the charge made by Soviet government and media, in a variety of conflicting and complementary versions, is neither here nor there: while these imputations need to be examined when considering the Soviet handling of the affair, they do not in themselves strengthen the case. Nor do they automatically disqualify the argument.

The investigation of the crash conducted by the International Civil Aviation Organization, which in many respects was serious, solid, and valuable, cannot be characterized as anything but a whitewash on this issue. The reasons for this are a matter of speculation, and while the influence of the United States in the ICAO is not likely to be irrelevant, they are not directly germane to the incident and crisis which are the subject of our analysis. The ICAO report focused on the Soviet allegation that the jet's departure time from Anchorage was delayed by forty minutes to coincide with "certain satellite orbital positions or passages." Its investigation usefully revealed that actually the departure time for each flight of KAL 007 was calculated separately so as to arrive in Seoul at 6 A.M. local time—a practice borne out by inspection of actual departure and arrival times for the preceding two months. (Nor is it apparent that the forty minutes would have made any significant difference in the ability of the space satellite to pick up data on each of its passages overhead.) The ICAO report thus found that since "there is no supporting evidence that the departure time of KE007 was planned for any other purpose or to accommodate an intelligence mission," the investigation "did not consider further the hypothesis . . . [of] a premeditated deviation from the flight plan route for intelligence gathering purposes."[30]

It is of course possible—indeed, sensible—to dismiss the forty-minute-delay argument and still entertain the "secret mission" alterna-

---

*In the absence of any reason to think otherwise, we will assume for the sake of this hypothesis that a U.S. government agency was involved, since there are no grounds for believing that an independent Republic of Korea intelligence effort would involve the overflight of Kamchatka and Sakhalin; nor is there any reason to believe that such an action would have been undertaken on behalf of any private individual or group. Logically, of course, such possibilities cannot be ruled out. Reference to a government agency is not meant to imply that an official or high-level approach must have been involved. Indeed, if true, such sponsorship is more likely to have been undertaken without the knowledge of Washington. If, on the other hand, such a mission required monitoring by sophisticated electronic equipment, the sponsors would have had to be in a position to control the use of the requisite machinery and personnel.

tive. Nor are United States denials of any intelligence complicity by the CIA necessarily conclusive.[31]

If, then, we consider the possibility that the pilot, and perhaps the co-pilot and flight engineer, had agreed to do a job for a government agency, we must ask why officials or agents of some arm of the United States government might have wanted the jet to fly as it did. Four possible— entirely speculative—answers come to mind. The flight across Soviet territory might have been intended:

1. To cause trouble between the United States and the Soviet Union at a time when their relations were possibly on the verge of some improvement.

2. To photograph or record some ongoing process or transmission from over Soviet territory that other planes, ships, or space satellites could not (or not as well).

3. To test Soviet air defenses or trigger higher alert levels in response to the jetliner's appearance.

4. To observe some unique or scheduled occurrence, such as a missile test.

These alternatives need to be examined further, but it should be re-marked in advance that, first, these four are not exhaustive alternatives— there might well have been objectives which have not yet been revealed, guessed, or reconstructed; and, second, the hypothetical decision to send the aircraft into Soviet airspace need not have been very smart; nor—if indeed it was a covert operation—would it in all likelihood have been cleared with any of the several agencies of the American government that have some direct responsibility for relations with the USSR.

Of the four possibilities, the first can be dismissed rather promptly as implausible. True, Soviet allegations have included charges that the American Administration was determined to heighten Soviet-American tension, sabotage the European peace movement, proceed with the de-ployment of Pershing and cruise missiles in Western Europe, wreck the arms control talks, and make Moscow look bad in the eyes of the world.[32] The timing of the incident was indeed suggestive. Some Ameri-can observers and occasional articles in the Western press have made substantially the same argument. Thus R. W. Johnson, a fellow of Mag-dalen College, at Oxford, in a lengthy exposé—full of shrewd surmises and gross misconceptions—after arguing that "the peace movement [was] dealt a crushing blow" by the incident, concludes:

> The whole thing is a massive and bloody attempt to manipulate Western opinion and stampede the U.S.'s allies into a new escalation of the arms race. It is impossible to say that [this] scenario is true. It is only possible

to say that it fits all the known facts and that the official U.S. version of events fits almost none of them.[33]

Whether or not the latter is true does not validate or falsify the Johnson version. To be borne out, it requires the Korean jet not only to be discovered, intercepted, and pursued by the Soviets but to be shot down and destroyed: both the effectiveness and the brutality of Soviet action, in this hypothesis, are essential to be counted on for the mission to make sense. Not only is there no basis for thinking that any American official planned it this way, but there were also virtually no precedents (more precisely, there was only one precedent—see below) of Soviet ground batteries or interceptor planes shooting up commercial airliners intruding into their airspace. There were no grounds for outsiders to count on such a Soviet response. It would also have required the crew to commit suicide quite deliberately—or else to have been singularly gullible. We may then dismiss this speculation as far more implausible than most other hypotheses and may safely place it quite low on the roster of possible and impossible explanations.

As for the remaining variants, they all share some common characteristics. In all three scenarios—unlike the first—at least some of the plane's flight crew (and its clandestine sponsors) would hope to get away with its overflight unnoticed and unpublicized. They would take care not to inform anyone else of their task and would act as much as possible as if no special mission were taking place; that is, they would report to ground stations and checkpoints what *should* have been the plane's position if the deflection over Soviet airspace had not taken place. How else can one explain the elaborate but manifestly and grossly incorrect reports from KAL 007 from points hundreds of miles off course when the correct data could readily be read off the instruments in the cockpit? To be sure, the co-pilot had to improvize temperature and wind strength and velocity (which may or may not have been those at the actual locations from which KAL 007 reported), since he could not know what these were at the checkpoint from which the plane should have reported, had it stayed on route R20. Indeed, later comparison of weather reports from various aircraft and weather stations made clear that KAL 007's reports were inaccurate. But had all else gone right, this posed only a small chance of detection and would have been a trivial risk for the cockpit crew to take, compared to the risk of flying over Soviet soil.

In these three scenarios, the flight crew would be deliberately blind to all indications of the plane's actual location—from its own instruments such as INS and weather radar, as well as signals from Soviet interceptors. They would ignore all radio calls other than from ground stations which believed it to be on track, including any calls from Soviet ground stations or interceptors on the international emergency frequency of 121.5 MHz.[34] And they would lower or extinguish lights so as to reduce the plane's visibility.*

Those inclined to believe that the United States had a hand in dispatching the South Korean jet over Kamchatka and Sakhalin are likely to cite various other bits of circumstantial evidence in support of their argument. While some (but not all) of these are not irrelevant, it is impossible to give them any specific weight in probing the alternative hypotheses. What are some of these ostensible clues?

There is little doubt that United States agencies have on earlier occasions used civilian planes for intelligence purposes—presumably for data gathering, as "ferrets," or (less relevantly) for purposes of transportation. In the nature of the case, most information is secondhand at best, but it appears that such use for reconnaissance purposes (for instance, on flights between Berlin and Moscow or over North Korea) was made largely before the deployment of space satellites capable of photographing ground installations in remarkable detail—a technological development that rendered unnecessary the risky use of aircraft for such purposes. It is true that the U.S. has continued to make use of such exceptionally fast and high-flying reconnaissance aircraft as the SR-71, presumably because it can observe or photograph objects the satellite may fail to pick up, but these appear to be limited to military aircraft. On the other hand, in the Indochinese conflict and on other occasions, U.S. intelligence even sponsored and supported entire "civilian" airlines to

---

*Whether one believes the plane had any lights on, and if so, when, depends on whom one wishes to believe. The official Soviet statements have invariably claimed that the plane flew "with extinguished air navigation lights and collision avoidance lights." This may or may not have been accurate during its passage over Kamchatka. However, the tape of air-to-ground conversations of Soviet fighter pilots over Sakhalin has three references by the pilot closest to 007 to "the target's" light blinking, and one to its air navigation lights being on. (Though the U.S. erroneously claimed the reference was to strobe lights, in fact according to the ICAO investigation the aircraft "was not equipped with white strobe anti-collision lights. The red anti-collision rotating beacons and the navigation lights were on when KE007 left Anchorage.") The Soviet "explanation" that the pilot was referring to another Soviet plane's lights is pure fiction. It is not impossible, of course, that the airliner flew without external lights over Kamchatka but during the final stage, when it was clearly being pursued and intercepted, it was blinking its lights, although this would contradict the view that the crew never noticed the pursuit or persisted in pretending that it did not know anything was amiss. In the Soviet television interview with the pilots, after the Ogarkov press conference, the Kamchatka fighter pilot was asked whether he had seen any light, and he affirmed that "the aircraft was entirely dark." The Sakhalin pilots were asked no such question. (*New York Times,* September 11, 1983.) Alain Jacob reported from Moscow that according to his Soviet sources the aircraft had flown with all its lights out until just a few minutes before it was shot down. ("Circonstances atténuantes?" *Le Monde,* September 10, 1983.) To judge by the transcripts of intercepted messages, the lights were visible at least sixteen minutes before the plane was shot down, and both before and after the tracer shells were fired by the Soviet interceptor.

serve its needs. While it is therefore safe to conclude that such instances had occurred and could perhaps occur again, it is not clear what probative value such information has with regard to the incident before us.[35] Nor is there in unclassified literature any certain indication that such use of commercial airliners has been made during the past ten years.

Even more tenuous are the implications of the U.S. government's intense and prompt reaction to the incident. On the face of it, it was a South Korean aircraft carrying nationals of a number of different countries, and the United States did not have an automatic mandate to "take charge." Yet the fact that it did, whatever one may think of it, in itself scarcely strengthens the case for U.S. responsibility for the plane's fate.

It has likewise seemed a strange coincidence that on the two occasions when, during the past ten to fifteen years, a foreign commercial airliner has illegally overflown Soviet territory, it has been a South Korean plane both times—and specifically deviating quite substantially from its flight plan to fly over the two most sensitive military areas of the Soviet Union: the Kola Peninsula in 1978 (as will be discussed at another point), and the Kamchatka-Sakhalin-Vladivostok area in 1983. Yet there is no way for us to push the argument further: it might have been a coincidence, and then again it might have been something else.

Similarly, there is no way of considering more than an odd coincidence the fact that the VHF radio systems—the so-called VOR—at Anchorage happened to be suspended for two days from early August 31 to September 2 (although U.S. authorities have apparently failed to provide an adequate technical reason for it). Similarly, the radar equipment at the most distant but important U.S. Air Force base on the Aleutians, Shemya Island, was not used to monitor civilian flights. Had these systems been used, it would have been easier for ground control stations to be better informed about the actual whereabouts of KAL 007.[36]

A small problem relates to the altitude at which KAL 007 was flying. As reported to Anchorage ground controllers, the jet was at 31,000 feet until authorized to climb to 33,000, which it reported reaching shortly after 1600 hours GMT (as relayed to Anchorage by KAL 015). The Soviet investigation report claimed that the "intruder" plane was first spotted (presumably on Kamchatka air defense radar screens) at an altitude of 8,000 meters (26,250 ft.) at 1951 hours Moscow Summer Time (1551 GMT), and that it exited Kamchatka airspace in the direction of the Sea of Okhotsk at 2108 hours MST (1708 GMT) at 9,000 meters (29,500 ft.).[37] If the Soviet reports of KAL 007's altitude were accurate, this might constitute a solid morsel of evidence showing that the co-pilot—who could obviously read off the aircraft's correct altitude—was wilfully providing false information in his position reports. However, not only have the original Soviet radar tracings not been authenticated, but it is commonly accepted that radar readings of a plane's altitude may be off by 10 or 20 percent.

The question has repeatedly been raised whether or not American and Japanese ground stations could have discovered—or did in fact know— where the jet was, and either could have warned KAL 007 or, if it was beyond radio range, could have warned Soviet air traffic control that the "intruder" was a scheduled commercial airliner. The implication, one must suppose, is that failure to alert anyone amounted ipso facto to at least a form of tacit American or Japanese support for the plane's mission.

During its flight, KAL 007 was under the control, first, of Anchorage, and then of Tokyo civil air traffic control. Once the aircraft was over the North Pacific, outside the range of radar stations, the plane's own position reports were the only thing civilian ground controllers had to go by. Radar data were available from military and civilian stations in Alaska, at the beginning of the flight, when KAL 007's deviation from the flight plan was still considered fairly insignificant. But, as the *ICAO Report* confirms:

> Once KE007 had passed Bethel, there was no means by which the controllers could have independently determined its position. From Bethel to KE007's destruction near Sakhalin Island, controllers had to rely on pilot reporting, the only available position information.[38]

Thus the civil control system, which was responsible for KAL 007's flight, cannot be considered delinquent. That leaves the military and intelligence networks. But neither American nor Japanese military radar installations routinely transmitted their observations to the civilian air traffic network: a serious communications shortcoming dramatized by this incident. True, "the U.S. Air Force operates electronic surveillance equipment and a radar tracking facility from Misawa Air Base on the northern edge of Honshu, and at Wakkanai, on the northwestern side of Hokkaido. The Japanese Self-Defense Force operates radar and electronic intelligence facilities at Wakkanai."[39] However, KAL 007 never came within the range of either Tokyo (Narita) civilian radar or, it appears, the American military installation at Misawa.

Japanese military radar at Wakkanai did indeed pick up an unidentified aircraft over Sakhalin—it was later identified as KAL 007—a few minutes before it was shot down. The Japanese technicians there had initially no reason to suspect that what they saw flying over Soviet territory was a foreign commercial airliner (which at that time had not been reported missing or off course). If, during the plane's final minutes of flight, Japanese radar observers had become alarmed (as well they might have), they might have asked the unidentified aircraft by radio to identify itself if its transponder was not already in use.[40]

All transmissions from KAL 007 had been routine. There had been no grounds for air traffic control personnel to suspect any trouble. Moreover, we are told that "the fact that reports of KE007 for NABIE and NEEVA were relayed by KE015 did not give rise to suspicion that something might be wrong. Such communication difficulties arise in this area and as long as position reports were received either direct from the subject aircraft or relayed by other aircraft or through Anchorage Radio (IFSS), operations were considered normal."[41]

It is a separate and intriguing question whether the RC-135 which, the U.S. acknowledged, flew off the Kamchatka coast, or other, even more powerful U.S. intelligence installations in the area, knew the jetliner to be off course, and—assuming the jet did not know—could have informed it (or its ground controllers) and thus saved it from destruction. The RC-135—a modified Boeing 707 with sophisticated electronic equipment—has been acknowledged to track Soviet missile tests and air defense patterns. The planes, writes one well-informed correspondent, "which are operated by the Air Force primarily for the National Security Agency, collect information about the abilities of Soviet radar systems, monitor communications between Soviet jet fighter pilots and ground controllers and observe the final stages of test flights of Soviet intercontinental ballistic missiles [ICBMs]."

> Several RC-135s that are equipped with even more specialized electronic gear [he continues] routinely fly off the coast of the Kamchatka Peninsula to collect performance data transmitted to ground stations by Soviet missiles. The Kamchatka Peninsula serves as the target, or impact zone, for many Soviet missile tests.
>
> Other, longer-range Soviet missile tests end in the Pacific. Intelligence officials said these, too, were monitored by RC-135s. The planes are equipped to collect missile telemetry, the electronic impulses that carry information about the flight and accuracy of a missile.... At an altitude of 35,000 feet, officials said, the planes have excellent reception at a distance of 150 miles.[42]

The RC-135s are only one component of a vast American network of intelligence-collecting in the North Pacific. The so-called Cobra Dane phased-array radar at Shemya can reportedly track one hundred objects simultaneously, with its 95-foot diameter antenna. Other U.S. electronic surveillance units are stationed in Japan. Specially outfitted vessels are routinely stationed in proximity to the Soviet coast. Under the circumstances, a strong case has been made—best argued and documented by David E. Pearson—that, quite independent of the Japanese monitoring of Soviet air traffic and communications, U.S. intelligence assets must have followed the KAL flight: they would have been delinquent if they had failed to do so. Indeed, it was later revealed that U.S. intelligence— presumably not only from RC-135s—had noticed an increase of Soviet air defense activity at the time the Korean Air Lines plane "intruded," but allegedly had no explanation for it and suspected Soviet maneuvers. In any event, as we have seen, the military and intelligence collection system had no mechanism for directly transmitting information to civilian aviation authorities even if it had been able to spot the cause of the activity its personnel observed.[43] The unclassified literature is ambiguous on whether the data would have been analyzed on the spot (as an early warning system required) or would have been transmitted for analysis by the NSA in the United States.

On the other hand, it is known that the intelligence gathering group in the Far East can contact high-level officials in Washington without delay by means of a secure communications network. In the wake of the KAL 007 crisis, two former U.S. Air Force intelligence specialists familiar with the RC-135 implied in an article that the capabilities of the aircraft— and, *a fortiori*, of the system of which it was a part—could have been used to "head off the tragedy" and that the whole system must have closely monitored the flight of KAL 007.[44] It is impossible to tell without access to classified information whether in fact any relevant message was transmitted to higher headquarters before the plane was shot down, and if not, whether this was because no analysis of incoming data was being made in real time or whether policies prohibited any action that would reveal the capabilities of the system.

Even if we conclude that at some level U.S. intelligence installations in the field may well have followed the flight of KAL 007—and the argument in favor of this proposition is strong—we are left with the same uncertainties as before. The answer to the question why such information was not promptly made known—while important—would not help us determine why flight 007 went astray, for even if some U.S. installations or personnel were aware of KAL 007's flight at the time it was taking place, it need not follow from this—though it may be true—that U.S. agencies or personnel had responsibility for the plane's mission or route.

If So, Why?

None of the above has shown conclusively that there was an American intelligence involvement in the airliner's flight. On the other hand, the available information does not allow ruling out such an intelligence interest in KAL 007's flight through Soviet airspace. We must therefore review the three remaining tasks which were hypothetically advanced above as conceivable objectives of such a mission—if there was one.

One explanation proposes that the overflight was intended to carry out clandestine data collection by means of photographic, radar, or sensor equipment carried aboard. The area overflown was unquestionably of considerable military interest, from nuclear submarine bases to ICBM sites to sensitive air defense and nuclear installations. And yet this fairly widespread and popular hypothesis seems to fall flat for several compelling reasons.

For one thing, it is not clear where in the fuselage of the B747 such rather bulky equipment could be installed undetected. To equip the plane in this fashion, it would have had to be withdrawn from regular traffic for at least a short time. Though there have been entirely unverified claims that a Boeing 747 without markings had been spotted at Andrews Air Force Base, Maryland, weeks before the fatal flight, no such action can be deduced from the available records (assuming they have not been falsified), and of the many persons who would have had occasion to observe it, no one has come forward with such information.[45] And the suggestion, made more than once, that this is what the forty minutes' delay in Anchorage was needed for is technically totally unrealistic. Moreover, the aircraft stopped at airports in different countries where service personnel—as well as passengers—of diverse nationalities and political persuasions had occasion to come near the plane: no intelligence operation would want to lay itself open in this fashion, and there is no indication that it did.

Nor is it clear that photography in the middle of the night would have been worth the risks involved in this or any mission—given the excellent and detailed photographs produced by space satellites—except perhaps infra-red pictures taken from much lower altitudes than the 747 would go to.[46] Everything considered, this alternative, too, can be set aside as highly unlikely. Nor has any credible suggestion been advanced as to what otherwise unavailable data—other than photography—could have been procured by such an overflight, except for one set of surmises discussed below.

By contrast, a second explanation—the possibility of the commercial airliner by its very passage through Soviet airspace triggering a higher stage of Soviet air defense alert, but not doing anything else, not collecting any data, not carrying out any other assignments—does present a realistic scenario describing an activity which would have been of interest to American military and intelligence people. It would also have been one easier to "sell" to the crew of a commercial airliner, as there would have been no physical evidence of any intelligence involvement and no need for the crew to do anything illegal—other than flying hundreds of miles off course. Hence it would have been easier to argue that the plane could innocently "get away with it."

It is worth noting that, after the Soviets advanced a variety of charges and scenarios in self-defense and counterpropaganda during the first week or two following the incident, it is this variant which, in one form or another, survived in the more serious Soviet arguments—e.g., the Soviet investigation report provided to the ICAO and the article summarizing the events published by Marshal Kirsanov on September 20—at least until the whole quality of Soviet arguments deteriorated to a new low at the time of the anniversary of the incident, one year later.

In its most professional variant, the Soviet argument links increased U.S. military and communications interests and reconnaissance in the Soviet Far East—and especially around particularly sensitive concentrations of strategic nuclear forces, ballistic missile submarines, and the air defense system, as well as Soviet command and control—with the orbit of an American reconnaissance satellite overhead which the Soviet sources identify as "Ferret-D." In this light, "the South Korean plane not only was performing an intelligence assignment but also was only one link in an overall system of major intelligence actions conducted, using a wide range of means, from Soviet Chukotka to the Maritime Territory."

The satellite, Moscow continued, "is designed for conducting radio reconnaissance in a broad range of frequencies on which the Soviet Union's radio electronic equipment operates." Given its revolution in orbit every ninety-six minutes, it passed three times over the Soviet Far East during the KAL 007 escapade. As Kirsanov put it:

> Naturally, the [initial] violation of the air border forced an approximate doubling of the intensiveness of the work of our radio equipment, something that the organizers of the provocative flight had counted on in their plan. All this was registered by the Ferret spy satellite.

The next time the satellite came around, the 747 was over Sakhalin, and the Ferret-D (apparently known abroad by its international designator as 1982-41c) "registered the operations of all additional Soviet air defense radio equipment that had been switched on in Sakhalin, the Kuriles and the Maritime Territory." In fact, he and later other Soviet officials argued, other U.S. planes and vessels were part of the same operation:

> Another RC-135 reconnaissance plane was patrolling along the Kuriles, an Orion plane was over the Sea of Okhotsk north of Sakhalin, and a

second plane of the same type was over the Sea of Japan. The American frigate Badger was on combat duty in the area of Vladivostok. There is also convincing information providing grounds for asserting that an E-3A (AWACS) plane, monitoring the flights both of the intruder-plane and of our fighters, was operating in the zone where the violation of Soviet airspace took place [see Map 5].[47]

There was indeed keen U.S. interest in and close American surveillance of the area in question, and it is impossible to dismiss the allegations of coordination between U.S. intelligence assets and the Korean flight, whether or not one links the flight to the reconnaissance satellite. It seems entirely true that satellites have come to perform valuable services not only in photographic but also in electronic intelligence. In many regards, the argument here is a more realistic and plausible one than most other hypotheses we have examined.

On the other hand, a number of old intelligence hands have raised serious objections. For instance, they have questioned the utility of such a mission. What the pros refer to as "tickling the PVO" is a game engaged in frequently and variously, by different types of military aircraft, and to a number of serious and independent American analysts the addition of a high-risk commercial airliner flight has seemed to be of questionable value at best.

To be sure, there are answers to this too. For one thing, U.S. military aircraft do not penetrate as deeply as the Korean jumbo jet did, and thus KAL 007 could be expected to set off Soviet radar and air defense systems not triggered in the routine games played by the two superpowers. For another, there is at least a suspicion that the Soviet confusion between civil and military aircraft (KAL 007 and the RC-135) was precisely what the alleged American sponsors intended to achieve.[48] Moreover, the fact that American analysts do not see, or do not wish to see, any rational mission which KAL 007 might have been asked to perform is hardly conclusive. Such retrospective "logic" may be out of place. Dispatching the plane over Soviet territory need not have been a smart or well thought-out decision. Ironically, despite the destruction of the aircraft and the death of all its passengers and crew, the flight was almost surely a virtually unique intelligence bonanza for the United States. But this, too, scarcely helps us find the answer, for—regardless of its fate—whether or not KAL 007 was intended to do what it did cannot be answered at this time.

The stage has become even more crowded with the addition of an hypothesis relating not only the reconnaissance satellite but flight STS-8 of the U.S. space shuttle "Challenger" to the alleged electronic monitoring. Though ingeniously collating a lot of material relating to U.S. electronic

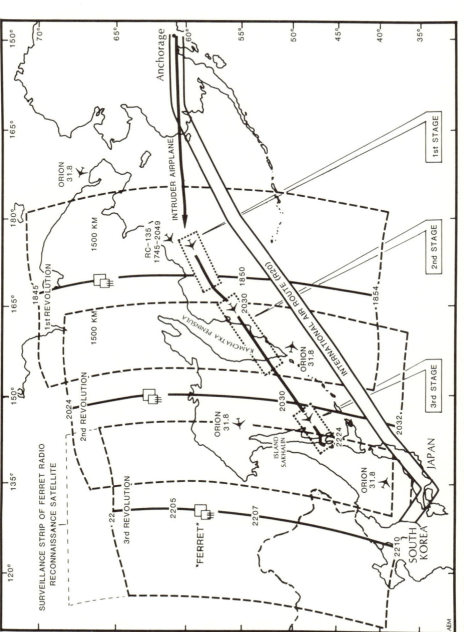

Map 5. Three successive revolutions of U.S. reconnais... re during KAL 007 flight (Se... map)

intelligence and testing of the Soviet air defense and communications network, the argument concerning the space shuttle's role in the operation has not been persuasive, and there are in fact technical objections to such a scenario.[49]

An amateur observer may reasonably raise questions to which only military or technical specialists can provide the answer. Thus, for instance, no cogent explanation has been given concerning the unique information on Soviet air defenses which a 747 flying at 35,000 feet could tease out which would differ significantly from already available information on the Soviet response to the customary approach of American fighter or reconnaissance planes to Soviet airspace without actually penetrating it, or which could be assumed to be relevant to potential future operational penetrations—say, by U.S. bombers. On the other hand, our inability to give proper answers to these questions does not destroy the relevant hypothesis. Indeed, even our failure to come up with a sound intelligence interest in the flight and its effects does not disqualify this explanation.

An additional and perhaps relevant complication is provided by the information—later leaked by American intelligence personnel—that on the night of the fatal flight of KAL 007 an important Soviet missile test was scheduled to take place. Unless one assumes that this datum was "leaked" as part of a U.S. effort to confuse the picture and mislead the outside analysts, the evidence seems clear that the Soviet test was canceled and took place either two or three nights later.[50] It is likely that the appearance of an unidentified plane—KAL 007—prompted the cancellation.[51] Was there possibly a connection between the missile test and the airliner's mission?

The test promised to be of exceptional importance for the United States. The SALT II treaty (unratified by the U.S. but substantially observed by both superpowers) allowed some modernization of missiles, but within specified limits. American defense specialists had expressed concern about a new missile which the Soviet Union had begun to test in early 1983—a three-stage ICBM which the U.S. first called PL-5, and then SS-X-25. While Moscow has claimed that it was merely a routine modernized version of the older SS-13, Washington had found it difficult to verify just what its characteristics were and was disturbed by Soviet encryption of test telemetry data. What was to be tested on the fatal night was an SS-X-25 fired from Plesetsk (near the White Sea) across Siberia to Northern Kamchatka.[52]

It would be natural for U.S. intelligence to seek to use all possible resources to monitor the test. Perhaps KAL 007 was to have had a role in this effort: this would explain many strange coincidences. But before we accept this idea, consider the counterarguments, which are at least equally persuasive.

First, if the flight crew had such an intelligence assignment, it could scarcely have been preplanned with such precision (especially as flight crews were rotated in fairly complicated patterns and the time of the missile test was scarcely set, let alone known to the U.S., very far in advance). Second, there is no technical information on just what a 747 could have picked up that other planes, satellites, and ships could not. To date, the only plausible idea has been the suggestion that the Kamchatka-Sakhalin-Vladivostok line of flight followed the path of a data link used in the open transmission of Soviet missile test data from Kamchatka back to regular (and more secure) Soviet land lines of communication from the Maritime Province to the European USSR.

Assuming KAL 007 was to have been involved in this monitoring effort, once the missile test was canceled (and presumably the RC-135 which had crossed KAL 007's path was sent back to Shemya once the cancellation became apparent through electronic intelligence), there was no reason for the airliner to continue flying over Soviet territory and thereby to endanger the flight's safety and the passengers' lives, and it could have been expected to stay over international waters.

There is also another bit of incoherence. It was predictable—or so it seems in retrospect—that the Soviet authorities would call off the missile test when a strange aircraft appeared over Soviet territory in the general proximity of the target area. Unless one assumes an unusual degree of incompetence, it is hard to see why the U.S. would want to dispatch a commercial jet into the relevant Soviet territory at precisely the time when it was bound to stop the test.

Different objections arise if, on the other hand, we pursue the possibility that the airliner had some other function to fulfill. If it was, in one form or another, to trigger Soviet air defenses, this made no sense unless powerful and sensitive U.S. monitoring equipment was alerted to follow the penetration. On the one hand, no low-level official or agent could decree and enforce such a priority. On the other, at a senior command level, the top priority was bound to be the impending test of the SS-X-25, to which—it is safe to assume—on that night the use of all equipment was dedicated.[53]

One objection made to the entire hypothesis is that, to trigger Soviet air defenses, it was scarcely necessary to use a civilian airliner with hundreds of passengers aboard. Part of the answer is that presumably it was precisely the innocent character of the flight that was to provide the most effective cover.[54] This does not dispose of the objection that using a drone might have achieved the same objectives at much less risk. Here the answer is presumably that (a) the construction and dispatch of such a drone would have imposed a substantially higher cost on the operation, and (b) especially if shot down, this might have been considered politically more compromising.

What, then, are we able to conclude? Many reasons have been advanced to explain the behavior of KAL 007. When all is said and done, we cannot yet be sure of the answers. It is in fact a fascinating puzzle. Both Moscow and Washington are likely to have additional pieces that are not yet in the public domain. Quite possibly neither capital has a complete or definitive answer.

There is no "smoking gun" that would clinch the argument. What we have shown is that most of the hypotheses advanced, then or later, do not stand up. But it is well to remember that it need not be the most plausible or the most rational explanation that corresponds to the truth: history is a fickle mistress, and logic may at times be a poor guide.

We have tried to show that the seeming likelihood of many of the available hypotheses is very low. Hijacking, jamming, instrument malfunction, and crew incapacitation would fall in this group. Not much more probable would be a secret mission to wreck Soviet-American relations. But they cannot be ruled out totally; nor can a supposed assignment to photograph or record something over Soviet military installations, which is a bit but not much more plausible.

While there may well be additional hypotheses that have not occurred to us or to others who have dealt with this incident, we are left, in essence, with three possible explanations: (1) a calculated attempt by the crew to save fuel—the least plausible and the least likely of these alternatives; (2) innocent error, of which at least two variants provide technically possible though humanly rather unrealistic explanations for what took place; and (3) an intelligence assignment, perhaps to trigger a higher stage of Soviet air-defense alert for U.S. equipment to record, or perhaps with a different objective. The relationship to the Soviet missile test is suggestive but has not generated any viable explanation. Similarly, the link to the reconnaissance satellite (or even the space shuttle) overhead is intriguing but also incompatible with the missile-test and other intelligence hypotheses.

There are some difficulties with all these explanations: none fits all the facts.* Given the political explosiveness of the issue, it is especially important not to jump to the conclusion that the whole thing was engi-

---

*It is possible to construct additional hypotheses which fit the known facts but for which there is no supporting evidence. In particular, it may be posited that the purpose—not the unintended effect—of KAL 007's flight must have been the postponement of the

neered by the United States unless there is good evidence to sustain this view. To be sure, the logic of that argument is strong, but that is a far cry from suggesting—even before a jury of dispassionate historians or fellow citizens—that this is indeed what must have taken place, especially since a plausible motive or mission remains to be supplied. By the same token, this possibility must not be ruled out simply because of the political embarrassment which its validation would occasion. In fact, it must be acknowledged that with the passage of time this argument, unlike all others, looms stronger than before.

If, then, some uncertainty remains, it is important to remind ourselves that the same—or even greater—uncertainty must have existed on the Soviet side when, during that fateful night, the decision was taken to shoot the aircraft down.

Soviet missile test scheduled for that night. To make any sense, this version requires a scenario such as this: U.S. monitoring facilities in the North Pacific are overtaxed by the need to assist in, and record, the effort uniquely conducted by the returning space shuttle (its return delayed by twenty-four hours to September 1) in coordination with an orbiting reconnaissance satellite, as well as the almost simultaneous test of a Soviet ICBM aimed at the Kamchatka impact area, with that flight taxing all available U.S. monitoring equipment. The solution that an NSA officer in Anchorage hits upon is to ask two acquaintances, piloting a South Korean 747, to do him a favor, assuming (correctly) that the appearance of a strange aircraft over Kamchatka would prompt the cancellation of the scheduled Soviet firing of the missile until another time, when the "Cobra" system could devote all its capacity to monitoring it. It must be underlined that there is absolutely no information to support this version.

3

How and Why: Explications and Explanations II

Why Did the Su-15 Do It?

To understand why the Soviet fighter-plane shot down the South Korean jet, we must ask first whether the destruction of KAL 007 was a
willed action or an accident; and if it was the former, at what level the
Soviet decision was made and what the decision-makers' mind-sets
were—what they knew or thought they knew, what they assumed, and
what they expected.

When faced with the need to respond to the "intrusion" on the night of
August 31/September 1, Soviet officials had to act without knowing what
the aircraft's purpose or objective was. Was the plane shot down in error or
by accident, or was the downing the result of a deliberate decision?

We would have to consider the destruction of KAL 007 to have occurred in error or to have been an accident: (1) if the Soviet air defense
command had been unable to distinguish between a civilian and a military aircraft, *and* if it would not have shot it down had it known that it
was a commercial airliner; or (2) if the top levels of the central political
leadership of the Soviet Union were not informed or consulted in advance, *and* if that leadership would have ordered not to have the plane
shot down because of the anticipated international repercussions of such
an action, whatever the military routine might normally command.

All the information available to us argues that, in these terms, the
destruction of KAL 007 was neither an error nor an accident. It was a
deliberate and intentional act. It also argues that (1) the Soviet ground
command which issued the order did not know that the target was a

civilian airliner, but (2) it did not much care whether it was or not: either way its behavior would have been substantially the same.

The problems facing anyone seeking to identify Soviet perceptions and behavior are markedly different from those we have encountered in trying to understand why KAL 007 went astray. What we have available from the Soviet side is the official account of the incident (or rather, the several quasi-official accounts), the flood of Soviet propaganda and counterpropaganda, and (unwittingly, as far as Soviet intentions are concerned) the tape of the fighter pilots' conversations before and after the airliner was shot down. We also have the later Soviet report to the ICAO, though not several important pieces of information which had been requested of the USSR in this connection.[1] Beyond this we have virtually nothing but some dispatches of foreign correspondents, a few leaks, endless speculation abroad—some informed, some less than enlightening— and a few interviews with Soviet officials and participants.

For any analyst who would prefer not to venture too far beyond the available evidence, all this adds up to rather little. The limited information makes it harder, and often impossible, to test alternative hypotheses. Of necessity, therefore, in looking for the sources of Soviet behavior in this case, we will need to fall back on a more diffuse familiarity with Soviet affairs and hazard some speculation. Regrettably, there is no better or safer course. Still, the contours of the decision are unmistakably clear.

Identification and Interception

What did the Soviets know, and when did they know it? Much is uncertain, but enough can be pieced together to make sense. At 4:51 A.M., Kamchatka time, a Soviet radar unit tracking the flight of an American RC-135 southeast of Karaginski Island detected a second, unidentified aircraft. As all Soviet reports have subsequently asserted, the two planes' "blips merged on the radar screens," and they were "monitored together for about ten minutes." Then one headed for Alaska (actually, Shemya Island), the other in the direction of Kamchatka, we are told. It has been the Soviet assertion that they could not tell which plane was the RC-135 and, in any event, what the second plane was. Under the circumstances, the Soviet investigation committee reported later, "the Area [or Regional] Command of the Anti-Aircraft Defense Forces concluded that a reconnaissance aircraft was heading towards the State frontier of the USSR."[2]

It is a fair surmise that spotting the unidentified plane had evidently led to the cancellation of the Soviet missile test which had been due to take place that night. An informant with firsthand knowledge reports that information on such radar sightings is electronically transmitted from all over the Soviet Union to a central wall map at national command headquarters; from there the relevant information—or the decision to cancel—must have been transmitted, perhaps by secure telephone, to the missile launching site near Plesetsk. In turn, it seems likely that, as soon as it had electronic evidence of the cancellation, the American RC-135 turned back toward its base. But what was the other plane doing there? As one analyst commented: "It is possible but hard to believe that Soviet ground-based air-defense radar systems are so deficient in signal-processing that they cannot identify an individual type of aircraft's radar 'signature.'"[3] Yet all we know prompts precisely this conclusion.

True, even if they had the schedule of regular commercial flights farther off the coast—as well they should have—they could not reasonably be expected to guess that this aircraft, hundreds of miles off route R20, was a South Korean passenger jet. In any case, this may not have occurred to the personnel if the atmosphere at the radar post is correctly conveyed by other Soviet accounts. According to the head of air defense aviation, "U.S. combat aircraft from the aircraft carriers Midway and Enterprise, which were 50–100 km south of Hokkaido, violated the border of the USSR nine times in the Kurile Island area. In addition, violations [of Soviet territory] occurred on July 6 in the Bering Strait in the Ratmanova Island area."[4] And in response to the Japanese Communist Party's call to disclose the truth, the letter of the CPSU Central Committee said that "on August 31 ... RC-135 flights were recorded in this area seven times."[5] Soviet interviews with the "radar scanners at the PVO subunit tracking station here on the desolate, rocky coast of Kamchatka" were to claim subsequently that, in the foggy and stormy weather, "hardly a day goes by without U.S. or Japanese reconnaissance aircraft being spotted flying along our borders. The American aircraft carriers Midway, Coral Sea and Enterprise cruise constantly along the coast."[6]

The natural thing to expect, then, was an American reconnaissance aircraft passing by and then turning away. But the unidentified aircraft did not fit any known pattern. Unlike the customary B707s (or B717s) going by, this one was headed straight for Soviet territory, for Kamchatka, and it was not about to turn back. Clearly, an air defense alert was called for; six fighters were scrambled to pursue the unknown "intruder." But this turned out to be a frustrating task, however much post-facto Soviet pronouncements would try to cover it up. It is hard to say whether he was joking, trying to excuse their failure, or reporting in full earnest, when a Soviet official remarked privately, months later: "It took us too long to sober up the pilots enough to get them to take off." As a subsequent

American intelligence study concluded, with good reason: "Soviet interceptors were unable to locate the plane for two hours. . . . Soviet ground controllers were encountering difficulty in directing the Soviet planes on courses that would intersect that of the South Korean airliner." Soviet fighters had a short range because of limited fuel tank capacity. Here they were going after an "intruder," a "target" (as they referred to it) flying at over 500 miles an hour at an altitude of some 30,000 feet. The probably accurate conclusion of U.S. analysts was, after the event, that the Soviet interceptors never got closer than within twenty miles of KAL 007 while it crossed Kamchatka.[7] Soviet journalists have claimed that Soviet air defense showed remarkable restraint, for it could have used surface-to-air missiles to shoot the unidentified plane down without any interceptor aircraft.[8] In fact, it is not clear whether Soviet ground crews would have known where to find it. Moreover, there were, of course, good reasons not to shoot it down, in any event: standing orders and Soviet rules of engagement called for getting an intruder to land, if possible; apprehending the presumed malefactors was presumably much preferable, both for intelligence and for propaganda reasons. But once it headed out over the Sea of Okhotsk, the airliner was again outside Soviet territorial airspace, and the interceptors turned back to their base at Petropavlovsk-on-Kamchatka.

At this point it is necessary to ask again whether the Soviet authorities knew that they were dealing with a civilian aircraft—a regular commercial Boeing 747 with some 240 passengers aboard. Initially this was one of the most disputed questions in the entire incident. While the information we have is not entirely consistent, the conclusion now does seem clear, and in retrospect most analysts seem to agree on it.

Whatever they may say, it is likely that the Soviet Union, and the Soviet military in particular, does not make as sharp a distinction between civil and military aviation as the U.S. does. In the USSR, of course, both civil and military aviation is government-owned and operated. In this instance, such a blurring is reinforced by their belief that the United States at times uses civilian planes for intelligence purposes, and by their knowledge that the Soviet Union does. Moreover, as we shall see, Soviet legislation on the handling of border violations also makes no distinction between civil and military intrusions.[9]

All Soviet accounts have stressed, virtually from the start, that they did not know that a commercial plane was involved. This may or may not be true, but the value of these assertions is diminished by their self-serving implications. True enough, there is a curious split in Soviet inferences from this fact. The official pronouncements, led by Marshal

Ogarkov and the military elite, insist that, while the Soviet command had no inkling that the "target" was nominally a commercial plane, this does not alter the fact that it was on an intelligence mission; and in a repetition of the same situation, the Soviet air defense forces would act precisely as they did. The destruction of KAL 007 was "not an accident nor an error."[10]

On the other hand, several Soviet civilian commentators, dealing with Western audiences, have insisted just as firmly that (in the words of one international relations consultant to the Central Committee of the Party) "if they had known there were civilians aboard, they would not have shot [it] down." Aleksandr Bovin, the influential Soviet commentator, privately told Western correspondents in Moscow he too was "150 percent sure" the plane would not have been shot down if the military commanders had known that it was a civilian aircraft.[11]

How the Soviet forces would have acted under other circumstances, neither they nor we can say, but there is good reason to doubt that optimistic assessment. Meanwhile, the view of experts, or would-be experts, in the American government, while divided, has shifted from the initial argument that "they knew" (or a more cautious "they must have known")—misleadingly spread by high U.S. officials in closed briefings—to the prevailing conclusion, after a second look, that "they did not know." If there is an informed consensus, it may be captured in the statement of an American analyst: "You end up with the idea that it was their business to know but that they didn't."

This view does contradict the flat assertions made, in the first days after the incident—and occasionally later—by people with access to classified information in Washington: whether they were misled or were on their part misleading others remains unclear. President Reagan declared that "there is no way a pilot could mistake this [aircraft] for anything other than a civilian airliner." Others even asserted that "U.S. tape recordings show . . . that the Soviet Far Eastern theater of military operations . . . 'knew the target was an airliner.'"[12] This is not borne out by any known facts or interviews. Yet it was the initial Soviet assumption that they were dealing with another RC-135. "A radar operator at an early point in the incident informed the air defense command in Kamchatka that he had sighted an RC-135."[13] Apparently, intercepted ground communications, too highly classified to be released by the United States, include orders to a SAM-2 (surface-to-air) missile unit stating that the target was an RC-135.[14] But one U.S. official apparently familiar with the material says: "It was never identified to the ground controller as anything but 'the target.'" That is congruent with the known tapes and transcripts as well as general Soviet practice.

An extensive review conducted in the U.S. intelligence community in the aftermath of the crisis concluded that there is no evidence that Soviet air defense personnel ever knew, before the plane was shot down, that their target was a civilian aircraft. According to the *New York Times,* this review included "transcripts of Soviet radio transmissions, radar impulses and additional intelligence data that American and Japanese officials refuse to discuss publicly."[15]

Now, one may well argue that they could and should have known. In fact, the "unidentified intruder" was flying much too fast to be an RC-135, which typically turns "lazy eights" while operating its communications gear. The airliner was also flying (until it was nearing Sakhalin) in a straight line—something the RC-135 did not usually do for a long stretch. But over Kamchatka there was evidently never any opportunity for visual sighting. Once it got to Sakhalin—still during the night hours—the Soviet interceptors never seem to have bothered to find out what sort of aircraft they were dealing with, nor is there any evidence that their ground controllers asked. When finally they sighted the four-engine aircraft from miles away, they appear to have stayed almost entirely behind and below KAL 007, thus depriving themselves of the best opportunity to identify it as something very different from what it had been assumed to be. From that angle, and in that light, the major difference between the 747 and the 707 was size, and the Soviet fighters do not appear to have come closer to it than two kilometers—and by then the fighter pilot was busy following instructions to shoot tracer bullets. He fired the two fatal rockets, a few minutes later, from about eight kilometers away. Moreover, not only is it "exceedingly difficult to tell one aircraft from another at night, since the observer has no point of reference for determining relative size,"[16] but, in the words of a knowledgeable survey:

> Calculations show that if the Soviet pilot in his Sukhoi-15 was indeed at around 8,000 meters throughout the engagement, then an RC-135 at 10,000 meters would have presented the same width to him as a 747 at 35,000 meters on the same line of sight.[17]

And while there was some moonlight, all this took place well before dawn broke over the Sea of Japan, in a sky with at least intermittent clouds.[18] (See Fig. 1.)

But then, a good case can be made for the view that, by the time the "intruder" was approaching Sakhalin, to the Soviet ground commanders in the Far East it really no longer mattered what sort of plane it was. They

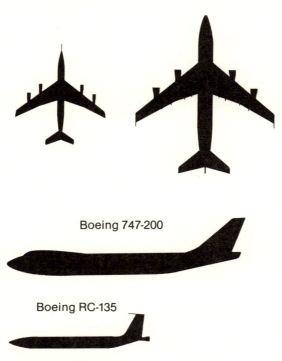

Left: RC-135 silhouette (wingspan 130 ft. 10 in.)
Right: B747 silhouette (wingspan 195 ft. 8 in.)

Boeing 747-200

Boeing RC-135

Figure 1. Silhouettes of RC-135 and Boeing 747

did not ask that question. If it was an unknown plane, so much the greater the potential threat which it might represent. It had gotten away with overflying Kamchatka; it had been teasing the Soviet air defense for two hours; it could not be allowed to go on doing the same thing. The order to the fighter pilots, before they were scrambled at Dolinsk-Sokol airbase (and perhaps other bases) on Sakhalin, was to follow the word of the ground controllers, who were in constant communication with them, whether it was to signal the "target" or to shoot it down.[19]

Meanwhile, no doubt, the officers in charge of each radar unit had communicated with the local air defense headquarters, which promptly informed the Theater PVO. Since 1980, the Soviet armed forces deployed within the USSR had been reorganized into five "theater" commands (each abbreviated by its Russian initials as TVD, for *teatr voennykh de-*

istvii): in substance, this amounted to a decentralization of the defense effort, with air defense and aviation placed under the theater command, presumably so as to be able to respond more promptly and effectively to threats and challenges in the area. The Far Eastern Theater was one of the five that were thus established, with its headquarters near Chita.

While the reorganization had apparently been under consideration even earlier, it is quite likely that the Kola (Murmansk) incident involving a South Korean jet in April 1978[20] had strengthened the hand of those arguing that the existing system was inefficient. Repeated rumors had it that some of the officers involved in the Kola episode had been cashiered; quite possibly "the commander of the Murmansk region [air defense] was dismissed because of the delay in intercepting the aircraft."[21] Clearly, that incident had "taught a lesson." That the Kola episode was painfully remembered was also suggested by Marshal Ogarkov's comment, in response to a question during his press conference on the KAL 007 episode, about how they had known that the jet had hostile intentions. KAL 007, he said,

> behaved in the same way as the crew of another South Korean airliner that violated the Soviet Union's airspace in the area of Karelia in 1978. The handwriting is the same. Moreover, this plane maneuvered, tried to escape from the Soviet fighters, and circumvented the zones of Soviet air defense missile forces.[22]

The Soviet air defense command, known by its Russian initials as PVO (for *Protivo-vozdushnaia oborona,* or anti-air defense), has three major branches: electronic detection, or radar; aviation; and surface-to-air missiles, with a total of over half a million men. In addition to the radar network of some 5,000 installations, it is estimated to have over 2,000 fighter-interceptors and some 10,000 SAM missile launchers.[23] Characteristically, all operations are controlled from the ground, and therefore the role of the radar system is, if anything, greater than in its American equivalent.

The assumption that the decision concerning the intruder aircraft was, and could be, made by an outlying and subordinate headquarters defies much conventional wisdom on the extreme centralization of decision-making in the Soviet system. Without wishing to undertake any systematic revisionism at this point, it might be suggested that, however great the centralizing impulse and the suspicion of "spontaneity," many decisions have to be delegated, and in this instance such delegation was part of an explicit and careful reorganization intended to improve the performance of military defense forces.

As a matter of standard operating procedure (at least as it was in the

1970s, according to a defector fighter pilot), foreign aircraft that penetrate Soviet airspace must not be allowed to get away.[24] Indeed, we know (and the Soviet authorities have restated) the standing orders, including an elaborate sequence of escalating warning signals, by which an intruding plane is to be made to land, from radio contact and rocking one's wings to firing tracer bullets along the aircraft's path of flight: these rules are in conformity with international practice. The new Soviet law on the border of the USSR, adopted in late 1982, which has been repeatedly invoked by Soviet spokespersons in defense of the decision to "stop the flight" of KAL 007, does in fact mandate the use of force, not exempting civilian planes.[25]

To be sure, such a stated policy must be clearly distinguished from its operational implementation. In all likelihood, there are classified guidelines for the several air defense commands (perhaps varying in content from area to area, e.g., from Eastern Europe to the polar region); and in any event, the application of stated directives in any given case must be left to the discretionary judgment of a regional air defense officer.

In this instance, theater headquarters near Chita was promptly informed of the "intrusion." Undoubtedly, Chita PVO reported the intrusion to national PVO headquarters in Moscow (or, more precisely, to the national command center reportedly located in Kalinin, northwest of Moscow).[26] One may surmise that simultaneously the incident was reported along KGB channels from its Far Eastern headquarters to Moscow as well. While we do not know whether Chita was merely reporting or was requesting instructions, the most likely scenario has the duty officer at PVO headquarters acknowledge the information—it is late at night, long after office hours, in Moscow—and tell the Theater PVO that it has full authority and standing orders telling it how to act in such a case; if there was anything further, he would be in touch. This corresponds, in fact, to what in military jargon is known as command by negation: the authority to follow standing orders unless overridden by higher command, something the national command center thus had an opportunity to do.

If this scenario is essentially correct, the decision to go after the "intruder" over Sakhalin was made—as Ogarkov in fact indicated—"by the regional command of the Air Defense Forces." There is nothing we know that contradicts this. According to Ogarkov, "the higher command were naturally informed at the proper time." Just when that "proper time" was remains somewhat uncertain. A Moscow correspondent later reported that "sources" said "the Soviet Far East command had been in direct telephone contact with top military officials in Moscow on several occasions prior to the downing of the plane. They suggested that the political leadership had not been consulted."[27]

The Far East TVD had a little time to get its act together while the potential "target" was still over the Sea of Okhotsk. During this time, apparently a number of messages went back and forth between the Kamchatka and the Sakhalin PVO, and between the TVD headquarters and Sakhalin. Before KAL 007 reached the island, at least four interceptors were up. They were keenly aware that they had little time: if the "target" crossed Sakhalin—a matter of minutes—and went off over international airspace again, they could not pursue it—both for reasons of international law and because the interceptors' range was limited by their fuel capacity. Ground control on Sakhalin was determined to do better than Kamchatka had done: if anything, this was a challenge it meant to live up to.

In the event, as we saw before, ground command *Deputat* followed the "violator's" flight path on its maps and accordingly vectored the three Sukhoi-15s and also, once it had approached, the MiG-23, so that they surrounded it. Most urgent of all was the fact that within minutes the "target" would leave Soviet airspace; if it then headed for Vladivostok (as it was assumed it would), this would constitute a new potential threat, but in the meanwhile it would also mean that the intruder had managed to overfly a second sensitive Soviet area without being "brought to account." Revealingly, Soviet statements speak of the airliner being about to "escape"—i.e., presumably about to terminate its violation of Soviet airspace; now, this could not be allowed! Both tracer shells and the two missiles were fired on explicit command from the ground. As a former Soviet fighter pilot recalled, his job is to concentrate fully on doing as instructed: "I must do exactly as I am told. I must execute perfectly," he tells himself.[28] And the pilot who did shoot the jet down later related:

> I fired four bursts of tracer shells right across his nose. At night they are visible many kilometers away. And this was right next to him. I dipped my wings. . . . But he continued to fly on the same course and at the same height. And I received the command—a precise and definite command.[29]

Whether or not his entire account is accurate, firing the missiles at KAL 007 was indeed explicitly ordered by ground control. It was virtually an act of desperation. By some calculations, when the missiles were fired the 747 was within ninety seconds of heading out to sea (estimates have ranged from fifteen seconds to two minutes). We know the rest.

Excursus I: Law and Custom

While not central to the dispute, legal norms—both Soviet and international—and compliance with customary rules and international practice have been invoked by all parties concerned. The problems here in-

thorities and aircraft made adequate use of proper procedures for interception. In general, the rules issued by the Soviet Ministry of Civil Aviation, and distributed both to Soviet pilots and to foreign airlines, conform to common international practice. The intercepting plane must signal by radio, flash its lights, and rock its wings, and the intercepted plane must respond with similar signals.

The Soviet instructions as distributed at home and abroad continue:

> An aircraft which is intercepted by another aircraft shall immediately:
> (a) follow the instructions given by the intercepting aircraft, interpreting and responding to visual signals;
> (b) notify, if possible, the appropriate air traffic services unit;
> (c) attempt to establish radio communication with the intercepting aircraft or with the appropriate intercept control unit, by making a general call on the emergency frequency 121.5 MHz and repeating this call on the emergency frequency 243 MHz, if practicable, giving the identity and position of the aircraft and the nature of the flight;
> (d) if equipped with SSR transponder, select Mode A code 7700, unless otherwise instructed by the appropriate air traffic service unit.[36]

Even the most generous reading of the evidence would have to conclude that, while some of these rules were followed, over Kamchatka and Sakhalin the PVO did not fully comply with Soviet, let alone international, law.

History and Context

What accounts for Soviet behavior? Having ruled out unintentional action, we must now seek to distinguish among different models of decision-making. If a "rational actor" model does not seem indicated — if only because the top Soviet leadership was never involved in a rational choice of a policy calculated to achieve certain specified goals relating to the jet — an "organizational process model" seems more congruent with the evidence at hand. Essentially, Soviet behavior followed certain preestablished organizational routines and procedures. It hardly conformed to the so-called "bureaucratic politics model": during the crisis, Soviet behavior cannot usefully be interpreted as the product of bureaucratic bargaining (though the handling of the disaster, after the fact, can be seen to reflect elite and bureaucratic politics).

On the other hand, other military establishments and air-defense units (such as the American) do not routinely choose to shoot down unidentified foreign aircraft. At the very least, we need, then, to add some intervening variables which in the given case create a predisposition to act in a certain way (without going to the extremes of a "systemic" model according to which the Soviet Union was bound inevitably to respond to an intrusion from abroad as it did). The following pages seek to explore some of the dimensions of such variables.

To anticipate a problem historians are familiar with: in retrospect, the course of history all too often seems inevitable. While the same observer might not have been able to predict the protagonists' next step, knowing what that step was often makes it easy—perhaps too easy—to link it causally to an array of explanatory variables. In fact, as we shall discover, we must guard against making the case so overdetermined that in our analysis we deprive the actors of any reasonable choice. Perhaps the only sensible answer is to be aware of the danger of such a distortion and to strive to be as realistic as possible in one's reconstruction of the setting and context of the events.

The decisions people make are shaped not only by the information they have at their disposal about the questions at hand, not only by their temperament and instincts, pressures and expectations, or by the institutional structures in which they are embedded, but also—though in varying and often uncertain degrees—by memories and precedents. It matters not that their memories may be not only vague but inaccurate, nor that the events they dimly recall may be quite inappropriate to serve as precedents for the cases before them. At times they may in fact not even be aware of what "scratches on their minds" have, indistinctly and obscurely, influenced their predispositions. More often than not, the past will have been amalgamated into some stereotypical platitudes of conventional wisdom with operational overtones.[37]

Soviet observers and advisers can fall back on such a collection of half-truths about Russian history, which have tended to influence the broader outlook of the Soviet educated strata, and especially the elite, regarding invasions from abroad, foreign encirclement, the meaning of sovereignty, and the "inviolability" of the native soil. Indeed, "outlook" may be too tame a term to use for an almost visceral response, for which the historical record (accurate or not, no matter) is but one of a number of sources. Most importantly, in recent years such a litany has been mightily reinforced by its systematic inculcation in Soviet schools and media.

In this reading, Russian history is seen as a sequence of responses to foreign incursions, from Scythians and Khazars to Visigoths and Avars, from Varangians to Huns, from Mongols and Tatars to Swedes and Poles and Turks, from Teutonic Knights to Napoleonic hordes, and so on down to 1918 and 1941. Russia—whether in its smaller, European configuration or as the continent-straddling colossus which it became in modern times—has had no natural borders. It has thus served as the arena of passage and the locus of ambitions for neighboring nomads and nation-states alike. No matter that the Muscovite princes and their successors, the tsars, had considerable appetites for aggrandizement themselves. What Russians remembered, or thought they remembered, was how often—as far back as recorded history began, it seemed—their land had been devastated, their society victimized, their homes ravished, their lives destroyed by invasions from abroad.

Russians were by no means unique in their widespread suspicion of the outsider, a trait which many foreign visitors to Russia have remarked upon; the Chinese and Japanese, to mention only two other civilizations, were at one time no less wary of the aliens; and many peoples—from American Indians to African slaves—could well argue that there were good reasons to be so. But in the Russian case, more than in most others, this sense that it was necessary to be on guard against the outsider was coupled to a perceived threat to territoriality and integrity. In folklore we can find defenders and champions of the "motherland" elevated to the status of heroes, models, and martyrs. And some historians would find in that ubiquitous perception—and repeated experience—of a foreign threat an abiding reason for the heavy concentration of power at the center, at the apex of the Russian state, for the widespread sense of reliance on the state for tasks which elsewhere more intimate or primary social units assumed, as well as for the secretiveness and insistence on obeisance which have been hallmarks of Russian political culture.[38]

What are we to make of these traits? How relevant are they to contemporary Soviet behavior? Though they were denied and assailed by the Bolsheviks of an earlier age, today they turn out to be congruent with the Soviet experience and the contemporary Soviet world-view. They have probably served to reinforce some of the deeply engrained instincts of orthodox Bolshevik ideologists, such as the effort to delineate more sharply the divide between "us" and "them," between inside and outside, between friend and foe (and the implicit notion that there is nothing in-between).

Starting with a world-view that posited an undying conflict between two "world systems," the Bolsheviks ushered in a period of history in which the Soviet state found itself surviving alone in what was perceived to be an inevitably hostile "capitalist encirclement." In 1918–20, it battled against the Allied intervention—something which Soviet political propaganda has inflated into a well-nigh universal onslaught on the Soviet system and (again) its territory and integrity. Time and again between the two world wars, Moscow spoke of preparations abroad to attack the Soviet state. And in 1941, Hitler's attack on the Soviet Union launched what was probably the most traumatic experience for its popu-

lation, not only in casualties and devastation but also because of the
perceived threat to its survival as an organic entity. Small wonder that
World War II still serves Soviet propagandists as the prime example of the
people rallying against the foreign foe, of concord of leaders and led, of
history validating so much of what the Soviet regime had sought to do at
so tremendous a price. The Cold War served to revive the Soviet regime's
manipulation of the threat from abroad. Indeed, some analysts would
argue that even in times of better relations with the non-Soviet world,
Moscow needs the image of the dangerous outside to justify its discipline
and controls, the mobilization atmosphere, and its fear of letting up and
letting go.

The notions of "enemy" and "border" are far more deeply embedded
in Stalinist parlance (and not parlance alone) than they are in its American (or Japanese, or British) equivalent. In the Stalin days, the allegation
of subversion from abroad—at times by enemies abroad ostensibly in
league with domestic enemies—was widely employed to explain away all
Soviet shortcomings and failures. And while a large part of the population correctly saw the effort as a self-serving exercise in fiction, something no doubt sank in to reinforce the siege mentality and the sense of
vulnerability. True, the use of these labels—and the need for their use—
has declined in the post-Stalin years, and the compulsive, embattled self-
isolation of the Stalin era has been replaced by a far-reaching search for
greater interaction with the outside world. Yet some of the underlying
attitudes—including the sense of "either/or," the global rivalry, and a
sense of inferiority—have turned out to be tenaciously persistent in at
least some parts of the population, and the elite in particular.

Inevitably, such an orientation has been reinforced by Soviet attitudes
toward, and the Soviet practices relating to, state borders and border-
crossing, the difficulty of entering and leaving the country, the formality
of passage in and out, the high importance attributed to the process and
to its symbolism (as shown, for instance, by the border guards, whose
actions and attributes are frequently extolled in the Soviet media). Borders are seen as the battle lines between civilizations—as surrogate front
lines.*

The unstated axiom underlying the image of a foreign threat is Rus-

---

* An astute observer remarked, not long before the KAL incident: "Russians have tradi-
tionally been subject to feelings of geopolitical vulnerability despite their country's vast dimensions. Moscow accords a high priority to the integrity of the USSR's perimeter, and 'frontier consciousness' forms a not insignificant theme in Soviet literature. Frontier consciousness
is especially acute in Northeast Asia, where the physical presences of China, Japan, and the
United States converge upon the Soviet Far East." John J. Stephan, "Soviet Approaches to
Japan," in Jae Kyu Park and Joseph M. Ha, eds., *The Soviet Union and East Asia in the 1980s*
(Seoul: Institute for Far Eastern Studies; Boulder, Colorado: Westview Press, 1983), p. 119.

sian weakness and insecurity. This was true in the days of Muscovy, and in its own way it has remained true to this day. In an oft-quoted litany, Stalin in 1931 evoked the image of a weak Russia throughout its history being beaten by foreign powers: the point was the commitment to the priority of breakneck industrialization and militarization of the Soviet Union that would henceforth make it impossible for the outside world to abuse Russia with impunity. That commitment remained and remains; the blithe vision of the inevitability of communism (a vision that has little operational relevance and inspirational power, these days) combines dialectically with the sense of an eternal uphill battle, seeking to catch up with the non-Soviet world, be it in industrial output, standard of living, military capabilities, or in science and technology. This also helps explain the great importance Moscow has attached to the symbolic recognition by the United States of "parity" between the superpowers—and as Moscow would have it, not only military but also political parity.

It is scarcely necessary to belabor the contrast between what has just been sketched and the American experience, American attitudes toward authority, and American values. At least until the nuclear age, the United States was relatively safe from attack and invasion—as Japan and Germany were to discover in World War II; the border with Canada—comparable in length to the Sino-Soviet border—is virtually open and undefended; millions cross the border from Mexico, whatever the rhetoric and the occasional attempts to impede the flow. For all but a handful of citizens, getting a passport to go abroad has never been a problem. In its own ideology, the United States became a superpower while extolling the spirit of individualism and, from Thomas Jefferson to the American cowboy, indulging in its suspicions of the power and purposes of government and politicians. And despite all the "red scares," security-consciousness has been a myth in a Washington that thrives on leaks and rumors. In spite of all the mirror-imaging by the two superpowers and their shared imperatives in the nuclear age, it is important to be mindful of the very different context in which Soviet perceptions are translated into policies.

To be sure, there has also been the contrary pull, both in earlier Russian history and in the Soviet era. The West has long been the object of tremendous attraction for many Russians—at least as a curiosity, more often as an object of envy, at times as a model, usually as the standard to compare all else with, and for some as the source of forbidden fruit: banned books, ideas, and information. Despite all their ambivalence and cynicism, the desire to travel abroad has been pronounced and widespread among Soviet middle-class youth. But for the Soviet establishment this only compounds the problems of access, contact, and control. And in a crisis it is typically the cruder instincts, the propounders of worst-case scenarios, and the confrontationists who have an advantage in making themselves heard.

What of it? It would be a mistake to say that the historical memories and cultural traits I have pointed to are necessary conditions for the behavior exhibited in shooting down the Korean jet; after all, other countries too have shot down foreign aircraft (though generally they have behaved afterwards in significantly different fashion) without having shared the same historical experience or culture; nor do they signify that Russians must always behave as they did here. Soviet official behavior has not always followed a straight line, by any means. I am suggesting that the historical experience—filtered and selective as it is—helped establish the context, the engrained orientation toward the outside world, the sensitivity to foreign incursions, and the pervasive insecurity that could be observed in Soviet behavior during the crisis. It thus serves as one set of the intervening variables that predispose the decision-makers toward acting as they did. What were some of the others?

The Superpowers Face-to-Face

In the superpower duel in which the Soviet Union and the United States have been engaged since World War II, each side has operated with a mixture of facts and fictions regarding the adversary. Whatever the reason— perhaps because of the historical and cultural background we have just reviewed, perhaps because the Soviet secret services themselves were engaged in analogous (albeit much easier) efforts in the United States, perhaps because Stalin wanted to believe that such an American effort had to be under way—Moscow soon began operating on the assumption that the United States was bound to conduct an intensive and extensive campaign to infiltrate agents into the Soviet Union, subvert whomever it could, soften up an assortment of groups, from "cosmopolitans" to "Zionists," and embark on a massive intelligence, surveillance, and propaganda operation targeted at the USSR. And, over the years, Moscow probably managed to uncover enough incidents, find enough evidence, get enough "confessions"—some genuine, some phony—to piece together a tableau of American intelligence activities directed against the Soviet Union that helped validate its worst fears and preconceptions.

Some of what appears, from time to time, in Soviet media on this subject is no doubt calculated to mobilize the population behind the regime, and to reinforce the official concern about the nefarious transoceanic adversary. It is no simple matter to tell just where the line is to be drawn between what is believed by those "in the know" and what is placed before the Soviet mass audience with an ulterior motive; in fact, many Soviet officials themselves are not quite sure what is truth and what is propaganda.

Here it is well to remind ourselves of one difference between our two societies. The same event which in the United States will attract passing mention in the press or on television, only to be soon forgotten by all but a handful of zealots and professionals, will be featured, repeated, inflated, and lacquered by the Soviet press and television, echoed by lecturers and propagandists, and displayed as one in a string of events which are all seen to belong to a logical chain of occurrences that unfold with a sense of historical inevitability. So it is that many incidents, thousands of miles away and all but forgotten in the United States, form part of the Soviet jigsaw puzzle of American intrusion: emigrés parachuted into Belorussia and the Ukraine, British and American businessmen in Moscow acting as go-betweens with informers, diplomats "caught red-handed" (as TASS is wont to announce the latest detection, real or imaginary), U-2 and SR-71 spy planes overflying the Soviet Union, and so on, in a chain whose length and absurdity vary with the degree of official paranoia and the state of Soviet-American relations.

If to this we add the considerable publicity given in Soviet media to the activities—real, exaggerated, or fictitious—of the U.S. Central Intelligence Agency around the world, typically accompanied almost daily by reports from Afghanistan, Nicaragua, or Lebanon, as well as unflattering cartoons, we begin to understand the disposition of the Soviet public to expect a virtually ubiquitous and unceasing American intelligence effort. Never mind that the Soviet Union, itself and through proxies, is engaged in activities scarcely less vigorous or more honorable around the globe. For the Soviet public, including fairly prominent public figures, the work of Soviet intelligence abroad—be it under the civilian KGB or the military GRU—is little more than a guess and an occasional rumor; the work of Western secret services is constantly kept before the public as if its existence both proved the Soviet system right and mandated a call to "vigilance."

Now, it is true that American efforts at information gathering have vastly expanded—not inside the Soviet Union but along its peripheries. Characteristically, this is not human intelligence but primarily the application of advanced technology and electronics. If there is not now the "capitalist encirclement" that the early Bolsheviks saw surrounding their state, there is in many ways its equivalent: an invisible web of electronic gear on land, in the air, and on and under the seas all around the Soviet bloc. If space satellites have given both superpowers relatively secure, unthreatening, and reliable means for mapping and photographing otherwise inaccessible areas, the perfection and proliferation of ballistic missiles provide the primary justification for the elaborate machinery of "elint," or electronic intelligence. Sensors, radar, photography, electronic intercepts of voice, Morse, and telemetry transmissions are all parts of this network, about which quite a bit has become known (even if not everything can presumably be revealed). By all accounts, it is a most impressive, intricate, and important system.

The Soviet Far East plays a special and perhaps unique role in this system, and as has so often been the case, the reason is twofold: on the one hand, it has in recent years witnessed a substantial expansion of Soviet military, naval, and missile capabilities (only in part directed against China, as Japanese observers have not failed to note); on the other hand, Siberia and the Soviet Far East have seemed to present major targets of potential opportunity for American planners and would-be strategists. (See Map 6.)

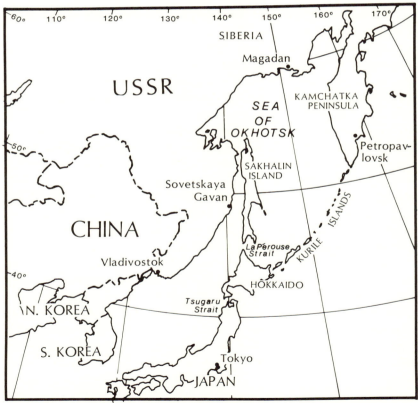

Map 6. Sea of Okhotsk and North Pacific Ocean

By most estimates, Soviet troop strength in the Eastern military districts of the USSR has grown from fifteen (in the 1960s) to about fifty divisions, with over 500,000 men—largely, of course, because of the tension with China—and of these, twenty-four divisions are in the Soviet Far East proper. The Soviets have well over a thousand military aircraft there. The Pacific fleet is the largest single component of the Soviet navy. Precisely Kamchatka Peninsula, Sakhalin Island, and Vladivostok—the three "targets" on the presumed track of KAL 007, as the Soviets claimed it—are the most important and perhaps most sensitive Soviet areas in this connection. Something like ninety nuclear-powered submarines are based at Petropavlovsk-on-Kamchatka, including apparently twenty-nine missile-carrying submarines. The Chukotka Peninsula, to the north, has been identified as the site for Soviet mobile missiles, which (some experts allege) could hit the United States. Kamchatka is also the impact area for Soviet ICBMs test-fired from the central part of the USSR. Sakhalin has at least six important airbases and a naval base. And, along with the port of Sovetskaia Gavan', Vladivostok is evidently the center of naval activities extending all the way to the Indian Ocean and the Persian Gulf. Sakhalin, Kamchatka, and the Kuriles all gird the Sea of Okhotsk, which serves as the sanctuary for Soviet submarines and other vessels—and, in particular, for the Soviet second-strike SLBM (submarine-launched ballistic missile) force—but which as international waters is also open to others and therefore tends to become a crowded area of potential friction, as do the few straits or potential choke points, such as LaPérouse Strait and (shades of 1905!) Tsushima Strait. Regardless of its purposes, the Soviet strategic buildup in the Far East has been formidable and unprecedented.[39]

But "the strategic factors that underlie Soviet paranoia" (to use Michael Klare's phrase) also include the reciprocal American interest in the area. The Soviet Far East may be relatively easy to cut off from the rest of the USSR, should it come to a conventional war. Soviet naval forces may be bottled up in the Far Eastern inland seas. U.S., Japanese, South Korean, and Chinese bombers could easily reach the most strategic targets in the Soviet Far East. Indeed—although this has not been official U.S. policy—at least two experts have urged making Siberia and the Soviet Far East a potential pawn for the U.S. to seize with conventional forces, something they claim the U.S. could accomplish far more readily than waging a conventional war in the Persian Gulf area or Western Europe. Needless to say, Moscow has not failed to note this proposal and to respond with venom.[40] Under these circumstances, an American analyst concluded recently, "the securing of the [Sea of] Okhotsk area against hostile penetration is the one truly vital task of Moscow's Far Eastern forces." Losing control there would be tantamount to seeing the Soviet deterrent, second-strike capability crippled.[41]

Far more direct and specific a reason for the escalation of tension has been the deployment of air defenses by each side and attempts by the other to test them. Both sides play this equivalent of the game of chicken—with the difference that usually the challenger at the last moment backs away rather than entering the adversary's airspace, though this too has occurred more often than either side is prepared to document. By one account, between January and September 1983, seventy-seven Soviet planes on their way to or from Cuba crossed into the so-called ADIZ (Air Defense Identification Zones) along the borders and coasts of the United States, which are formally off-limits to foreign aircraft. In turn, it is alleged, altogether more than nine hundred Soviet ground-to-air missiles have been fired (without a single hit!) in Soviet efforts to chase off intruding American planes—typically, fast-flying fighters.[42]

In addition, the U.S. has of course deployed the aircraft and vessels needed for its electronic surveillance: this is the function of the RC-135s as well as of SR-71s, AWACS, and other planes, whose continual patrols on the perimeter of the Soviet Far East create an atmosphere of mutual irritation and permanent alert.

To be sure, the incidence of crises stemming from the encounter of military aircraft—or from their crash—appears to have gone down dramatically since (1) aerial guidance systems have improved technologically; (2) satellite photography has reduced the incentive for either side to penetrate or overfly the other's territory; and (3) particularly "interesting" events such as missile tests can be elaborately monitored from outside the launching nation's airspace. The Gary Powers flight—and crash—of the U-2 in 1960 was, of course, the most traumatic and well-publicized event, reference to which remains frequent in Soviet enumerations of United States misdeeds and intrusions.

That era is past. Moreover, in the 1960s and '70s the Soviet Union learned, somewhat reluctantly, to accommodate itself to the flight of literally thousands of foreign aircraft, each year, over its territory as part of a regular network of international civil aviation. And, as Moscow has accurately insisted since the KAL 007 incident, given the many thousands of miles flown each year by foreign planes over Soviet soil, on the whole the experience has been remarkably safe and lacking in crises—whatever the special care and caution which foreign pilots make certain to exercise over Soviet territory.

Excursus II: Precedents and Analogs

KAL 007 was not the first aircraft to be shot down by another state or by adversary forces in peacetime. There are at least twenty-eight known incidents involving military aircraft—all between 1945 and 1960—and at least ten involving civilian aircraft, none nearly so costly in human lives as the crash of KAL 007. Several of the military encounters, in the early 1950s, were also in the Far East, in the area between Kamchatka and Japan.[43]

One of the incidents curiously foreshadowed some of the aspects of the KAL 007 disaster. In September 1958, a U.S. EC-130 crashed near Leninakan, in Soviet Armenia. As it later turned out, the aircraft "had been carrying electronics specialists and special equipment for receiving at close range the signals of Soviet radio transmitters," and the plane, based in Turkey, had apparently crossed the Soviet border "in order to get into immediate proximity of Soviet radar installations."[44] Six of the plane's crew were killed, the other eleven missing. Moscow denied having had a role in its fate, until the U.S. (having pressed its case, in vain, by quiet diplomacy) released the taped transcripts of conversations between a Soviet MiG pilot and ground control, which ordered the pilot unmistakably to "Attack, attack!" Soon the pilot reported that "the target" had been hit and was burning and going down. Moscow promptly called the recording a "fake" and a "forgery," and the fate of the missing men has remained unknown.[45]

In 1955, a commercial El Al airliner, en route from London to Tel Aviv, wound up over Bulgarian territory. Two Bulgarian fighters—MiG 15s—pursued the Constellation and used their cannons against it. The plane crashed, killing all fifty-eight persons aboard. Subsequently, the Bulgarian government apologized and agreed to pay compensation.[46]

The incident most costly in human lives (prior to 1983) and perhaps most comparable to the KAL 007 disaster was the shooting down of a Libyan Airlines Boeing 727 by an Israeli Phantom F-4E in February 1973, killing 108 of the 116 passengers aboard. The destruction occurred over the Sinai Desert, which Israel considered a war zone. Israeli Defense Minister Moshe Dayan defended the action, claiming that the French pilot of the Libyan plane had acted strangely and had refused to follow Israeli instructions to land at the nearest airbase; Prime Minister Golda Meir justified it by citing intelligence reports that Arab terrorists would try a suicide raid on Israel; and the Knesset voted the Israeli pilots a clean bill of health. Foreign Minister Abba Eban was alone to dissent—until investigation revealed that the pilot of the Libyan plane had thought the Israeli interceptors to be friendly Egyptian escorts, and that in any event he had merely overshot Cairo and was on his way back there. Then the Israeli government rather reluctantly reversed itself, expressed its regret, and offered a payment to the victims' families.

This incident, which at the time attracted remarkably little attention in the United States, provoked two sets of comments after the 1983 Korean airliner disaster. Moscow radio cited it as another example of American protection of "Zionist air piracy."[47] On the other hand, Robert Scheer, writing in the *Los Angeles Times,* drew some astute comparisons with the KAL 007 crisis and reached conclusions that anticipate a point to be made later on. Did Soviet behavior in shooting down the plane reveal "the Soviet Union's aggressive worldwide designs and its refusal to abide by commonly accepted standards of civilized behavior? If the answer [Scheer wrote] is that the dastardly Soviet behavior in this incident is a necessary result of the inevitable working of their totalitarian system, then how does one explain quite similar behavior on the part of one of the world's most democratic societies?" The Israelis, too, first stonewalled and then rallied to defend the behavior of their pilots. To be sure, unlike Moscow, they then apologized. Still, Scheer concludes that

> Clearly, the compelling lesson of both incidents is that when nations, whether through choice or necessity, adopt a violent, hair-trigger approach to national security, the safety of all is put at risk.[48]

The remaining instances in the 1970s involved groups of insurgents or exiles. In October 1976, Cuban anti-Castro counterrevolutionaries placed a bomb aboard a Cuban airliner during a stop at Barbados: when it went off, it killed seventy-three people on board. And Zimbabwe insurgents, under Joshua Nkomo, shot down two Air Rhodesia Viscount airliners—one in 1978 and another in 1979, resulting in thirty-eight deaths in the first and fifty-nine deaths in the second crash.

But the most relevant precedent, and one which may well have played a part in shaping Soviet responses in 1983, was the downing of another South Korean commercial airliner by Soviet fighters over another militarily sensitive area. On April 20, 1978, flight KAL 902, a Boeing 707 on a regular run from Paris to Seoul (with a refueling stop in Anchorage), with 110 passengers and crew on board, apparently found itself seriously disoriented. Seemingly, the plane's navigation system (allegedly its gyroscope), in the days before the INS was widely used by commercial planes, malfunctioned to the extent of sending the aircraft more than one thousand miles out of its way off the Polar route south over the Soviet Union, at a 112-degree turn, straight on to the Murmansk (Kola) Peninsula—a development which has been called "the worst navigational error in modern aviation history." There the Korean airliner flew for some two hours over sensitive military installations before it was intercepted by a Soviet Su-15 fighter, which signaled it to land at the nearest airfield. The South Korean pilot later claimed that there was no way of establishing radio communication because the Boeing's and the Sukhoi's radios operated on different frequencies. When the plane did not respond, the Su-15 fired its cannon at the plane, hitting one wing and the fuselage, causing some damage and considerable havoc, and killing two passengers. The KAL pilot finally managed to put the plane down on a frozen lake near the city of Kem, south of Murmansk.

American officials have privately indicated that communications intercepts show an explicit exchange between the Soviet fighter pilot remonstrating that the intruder was a civilian plane carrying passengers, and ground controllers telling him to proceed with shooting it down nonetheless. According to one version, the order was "to force the plane down by firing on it, but to bring it down in a condition that would permit a thorough examination." In this bizarre incident, which has never been adequately explained, the Soviet Union did recover the plane's "black box"—its flight recorder—but never made public any of its contents. Nor did Moscow charge the Korean crew with any subversive or intelligence intentions (though it claimed that the plane had no identification marks). Within ten days, Moscow announced that the pilot and copilot had admitted their guilt of violating Soviet air law and failing to obey the instructions of Soviet fighters to follow them to the nearest airfield, and that therefore the Soviet Union, "guided by principles of humaneness," limited its action to expelling them from the Soviet Union. The passengers were airlifted out and allowed to leave, while the Boeing 707 remained where it had crashed, presumably soon to be dismembered by Soviet personnel. Curiously, the pilot was never reprimanded or punished by KAL. The reaction of all governments and media concerned was subdued and moderate. It is ironic, in retrospect, that after the incident the London *Guardian* should have editorialized: "There ought to be a foolproof system, short of gunfire, whereby a military aircraft can warn a civilian one that it is committing an offense."[49]

What the Soviet authorities knew or suspected about the plane's purpose remains unknown, though a hint may be contained in Marshal Ogarkov's remark that KAL 007 was suspect because it behaved just as the Korean Air Lines plane had in 1978! What obviously bothered the officers in charge of the Soviet air defense forces after this incident was the fact that an unarmed civilian plane—there was no doubt here about the fact that it was a commercial aircraft—could with impunity fly over Soviet territory, and especially over sensitive military and naval installations which studded the Murmansk area, for two hours without being picked up or forced down. That experience was to leave its mark on Soviet policies and personnel.

It is equally true that scheduled Soviet-bloc passenger aircraft have also repeatedly entered airspace beyond their assigned tracks, in at least some instances clearly to fly near or over installations of military interest. The U.S. has repeatedly charged Aeroflot with flying unauthorized routes over the United States, and on at least one occasion imposed a two-week suspension of Soviet flights as a result. Shortly before being barred from landing in the United States (in response to the imposition of martial law in Poland), two Aeroflot planes were reported to have flown over the naval shipyards at Groton, Connecticut, including once when the first Trident nuclear submarine was being launched. LOT and CSA, the Polish and Czechoslovak airlines, have similarly been accused by the United States of flying over zones marked off-limits to them. There have also been reports of Cubaña airliners on the way from Havana to Canada passing over U.S. soil, and U.S. air force bases in particular. The United States has apparently never fired at any of these passenger flights or forced them down.

Political and Bureaucratic Culture

Between long-range historical images and perceptions at one end and the immediate precipitants at the other, one other cluster of variables remains to be identified: Soviet political and bureaucratic culture.

One may, of course, argue that the decision to shoot down the intruding aircraft was a narrow, technical, military one, taken by people doing their job. In that case, broader considerations—cultural, political, and historical—would be deemed irrelevant and out of place. But if we seek to place the individual actors in a wider institutional, cultural, and systemic setting—and if we ask why their "job" was so defined—we must recognize that their values and their way of operating are bound to have been shaped by the entire sociopolitical environment. This is not contradicted by the regrettable circumstance that we cannot properly demonstrate the relevance of these vaguer and broader traits nor quantify their relative weights in the total balance of causality.

A number of characteristic traits of official Soviet behavior seem to be related to the pervasive sense of weakness and insecurity. Observers have repeatedly commented on Soviet (and, more generally, Russian) oversensitivity to "humiliation," the fear of being pushed around, the neurotic avoidance of anything apt to make one the laughingstock of others. In our case, the fear of being seen as having failed would extend, first, to the individual actor, but second, to the organization—say, the PVO—and beyond it, to the country.[50]

Not unrelated is the tendency toward *perestrakhovka*—"over-insurance." The mind-set that acts on the assumption that it is better to be safe than sorry finds expression in many ways, including the bureaucratic tendency not to give a subordinate or a client the benefit of a doubt, the tendency to protect oneself from all possible criticism at the expense of others, the tendency to overdose patients to make sure an illness is cured (efficiency), and the tendency to confine convicts for longer rather than shorter terms. This attitude also means not taking initiatives in departing from the stipulated rules and regulations, especially if you are being watched. Shooting down the unknown intruder meant going by the book: it was a safe way for the Far East PVO commander to protect his *zadnitsa*.

Other features would become more obviously apparent if we looked more closely at the handling of the episode after it occurred: here we would encounter a characteristic syndrome of stonewalling, buck-passing, withholding and fabricating evidence, *lakirovka,* and what is commonly known as *vran'io*—an enthusiastic, at times cavalier, at times excessively imaginative manipulation of the truth. One might also point to institutional and political as well as cultural barriers to information flow and to innovation in Soviet society.

My argument is not that these are in any sense uniquely Russian, or Soviet, attributes, nor that they are universal in the USSR. What is being posited is that, for a combination of reasons too complex to investigate further in the present context, these traits do appear to be sufficiently pronounced, widespread, and significant in the Soviet Union to identify them as relevant to the behavior of the actors in the Korean jetliner drama.

Another strand which strikes me as powerful and pervasive in the Soviet reaction to events is the fear of losing control. This can be traced back to Lenin's fundamental choice in opting for "consciousness" (ostensibly by the most advanced Party members, which in fact amounts to control by the most powerful) over "spontaneity." It foreshadowed the triumph of institution over individual. By the time Stalin, in the 1930s and 1940s, sought to eliminate all vestiges of pluralism and heterogeneity not only in politics and economy but even in culture and society, the leadership had arrogated to itself the authority for complete social, political, and economic engineering. Complete control was the obvious precondition for such a revolutionary transformation from above. This was one reason why no dissent could be tolerated—not only logically and ideologically, since there was but one truth, but above all viscerally—nor could anything be allowed to intrude from outside to interfere with the "building of socialism." By the early 1950s, the Soviet Union was just about hermetically sealed off from the outside world. The economic policy of autarky—self-reliance—went hand in hand with this view. To be sure, in the post-Stalin days both this practice and the attitudes that underlie it have moderated some, and at times the implications of this outlook can be subordinated to other priorities—such as sharing foreign technology and skills—but there remains a fundamental orientation which sees in even an inadvertent crossing of Soviet airspace both a challenge to and a manifest failure of Soviet control. And that, as has been suggested, is another area of intense Soviet sensitivity: the fear of being put down, humiliated, or ridiculed.

Hand in hand with the obsession with control has gone the elaborate embroidery of the myth of Soviet infallibility. Neither to your own people nor to the adversary who watches and listens may you ever admit any error, any failure, any doubt that might make you appear less than fully committed, all-knowing, or omnicompetent. You may not admit anything that might lead people to question not only whether you are in control but whether you are best qualified to lead and whether the doctrinal basis of what you are doing is adequate or sound. Were cynicism not already so pervasive in the USSR, the legitimacy of the regime and its official belief system might be put in doubt. Only after a leader is ousted or dead may you heap on him the blame for failures past, thereby clearing your own slate; only by blaming the hostile outside world can you shift responsibility away from yourself. Moscow does not apologize. In a unique (but psychologically very sound) mix of inferiority and superiority, a combination of infantile stubbornness and superpower arrogance, the culture prompts a defensive instinct: for the Soviet Union, being a superpower means never having to say you're sorry.

Guesses and Gaffes

The way the Soviet authorities dealt with KAL 007 reflected a rigid mentality of "going by the book"—following the rules in a defensive, almost mindless fashion. It ignored not only the human tragedy but even the political costs of the action. It neglected the possible gains of "capturing" the plane's crew and equipment if indeed there was anything to seize or reveal that Moscow would have wanted to exhibit to its own people and to the outside world, much as it had done with Gary Powers and the U-2, a generation earlier. True, by the time the missiles were launched, there was no more chance (at least over Sakhalin) of compelling the intruder-plane to land at a Soviet airstrip. The alternatives were either letting it get away or killing it. The choice was clear.

The sequence of events was, from all appearances, the result of military decisions from beginning to end. Given its effect, it is not surprising that the destruction of KAL 007 should have led to some friction between civil (Party and state) and military elements in the Soviet elite—friction which analysts abroad have at times exaggerated and at other times ignored altogether. An ostensible Soviet general, Grishin, who was said to have defected to Turkey in October, was reported to have remarked that there had been friction between the Communist Party and the army after the Korean airliner was shot down.[51] More significant and direct evidence was provided by an interview which Viktor Afanas'yev gave to BBC during a visit to Britain, a few weeks after the episode. Afanas'yev, as editor of *Pravda,* a member of the Central Committee of the CPSU, and a full member of the Academy of Sciences of the USSR, can be taken to represent the civilian establishment. After repeating some standard Soviet arguments, he was asked why it had taken the Soviets so long to admit what had occurred. He answered:

> I think that in this respect our military people are guilty. . . . That's what I think. That's my own simple version. I can't claim to know. I wouldn't say I was very pleased with our first reports.

Asked whether decisions which could have such disastrous consequences should not be taken by political leaders, he responded:

> I think that our government and our party will certainly draw some conclusions—perhaps, as you say, political, and may do something of this kind. But nobody, anywhere, anytime should be deluded into thinking that we, a great country, a big country, will allow shameless, flagrant violations of our frontiers.[52]

These remarks reflect both the unwitting tension between civilian and military and the underlying siege mentality which both groups share. One can speculate about the scope and seriousness of the tension, but one thing the evidence does not warrant is the sort of distortion which led, in the wake of the Korean jetliner episode, to a widespread argument—at least in Washington—that the Soviet "marshals" were fixing to take over from an ostensibly "soft" or indolent Party elite.

Perhaps because of the fact that Yuri Andropov was out of public sight since before the jetliner episode, perhaps because of the unusual role which Marshal Ogarkov and other senior Soviet military commanders played in "explaining" and justifying the event, there emerged in the

West, and especially in Washington, a thoroughly mistaken view that the military was in effect challenging—or double-crossing—the Politburo. In one variant, the armed forces, eager to have higher budgetary allocations, were intent on sabotaging arms-control negotiations, which were perceived as being promoted by the Andropov regime. In another, the military brass, impatient with the seeming inability of the Party leadership to take drastic steps which were needed in the economy, in military policy, and in Soviet society, had simply begun to push the civilians aside.[53]

To be sure, the visibility which the top military commanders acquired—not only in the aftermath of the KAL 007 crisis but also on other questions of concern to the armed forces, such as those relating to the imminent deployment of U.S. Pershing and cruise missiles in Western Europe—was virtually unprecedented. But under the circumstances, there was apparently a tacit (or perhaps even an explicit) agreement: the party leadership preferred the military commanders to take the heat and offer technical details, with which they were more familiar; the senior officers may well have welcomed the unusual limelight of press conferences, television coverage, and virtually limitless space in the Soviet press. And, to avoid all misapprehension (or so Moscow thought), on such occasions Marshal Ogarkov or his equivalent was invariably flanked by high Party and diplomatic officials.

One thing that clearly did not take place was an attempt by the "marshals" to take over or push the civilians aside. That responsible American officials and careful reporters should have seriously considered such a prospect tells us more about the low level of political literacy in the United States regarding the Soviet Union than about the state of Soviet politics. Insofar as the Korean airliner figured in these speculations, the role of the military was precisely what it should have been expected to be. The S.O.P. had never foreseen convening a Politburo meeting (even if it had been possible) or consulting the general secretary (even if he could have been reached) in case of a foreign aircraft's penetration into Soviet airspace. After the event, the Politburo no doubt did discuss the matter—both the incident itself and its handling by the Soviet authorities and media—but that is a very different matter.

Particularly silly was the theory—circulated in Washington and seriously reported by several national newspapers and weeklies—that the military ordered KAL 007 shot down to embarrass Andropov and torpedo the looming improvement in Soviet-American relations. This was just about the counterpart to the radical conspiracy theory according to which American hawks sent the airliner over Soviet territory to be shot down so as to prevent a Soviet-American rapprochement. Suffice it to say that there is not the slightest shred of evidence or logic to support this view. This fact is not altered by the dismissal of Marshal Ogarkov from his position as chief of the General Staff, a year later. While the reasons for his replacement and the circumstances which led to it remain unclear, it is most unlikely that they related to the destruction of KAL 007.

No less erroneous and predictably misleading was the widespread assumption, during the first days after the disaster, that the destruction of KAL 007 represented a policy decision taken at the very top level of Soviet power. The papers were rife with speculation as to what Andropov was up to. Within the Administration, one gathers, papers were being drafted on what the Kremlin was trying to signal by such behavior as shooting down a South Korean jet. In fact, it was, of course, not the result of any such policy decision; it told us nothing of Soviet intentions; and it did not indicate any change of Soviet behavior—at least not until the American response became apparent. Here again the U.S. reaction showed a regrettable, counterproductive ignorance of Soviet affairs, as costly as it was unnecessary.

On balance, it must be said that the Soviet air defense system performed poorly. One knowledgeable journalist has hypothesized that, to judge by Soviet behavior, "there is a large gap in Soviet radar coverage of its northern airspace in East Asia, and even more so in fighter coverage."[54] The chief of staff of the U.S. air force, Gen. Charles Gabriel, found Soviet air defense, as manifested in this crisis, to have been marked by confusion and rigidity.[55] Even on a more technical level, Soviet interceptors did not go aloft until about forty-five minutes after the "unidentified" plane appeared on Soviet radar. Over Sakhalin, even though the fighters took off before KAL 007 was over land, it still took them twenty-three minutes before they reported sighting it.[56] The PVO both misidentified the aircraft (or failed to identify it) and, over Kamchatka, let it get away. Small wonder that stories soon began to circulate that personnel changes were taking place in the Far Eastern PVO, including the removal of several senior officers in the theater command.[57] Yet when it comes to the ultimate decision to "stop the flight" of KAL 007, the Soviet ground controller went by the book.[58] As William Hyland commented, the tragedy was that the system worked.

4

Consequences and Conclusions

The way each superpower behaved during the crisis and the way it managed the story of the disaster, in the following days and weeks, laid bare some fascinating similarities and important differences between the two systems. We have looked elsewhere at each country's crisis behavior; here we want to focus briefly on the handling of the incident after it occurred. A helpful framework for such a survey is a comparison of the different objectives which the authorities in the Soviet Union and in the United States pursued at this stage.[1]

Though no responsible government official may have articulated or ranked them in this fashion, U.S. practice suggests the following rank order of priorities in the handling of the jetliner "story" on the part of American authorities:

1. Tagging the Soviet Union as the criminally responsible party, guilty of mass murder and the violation of moral and legal norms accepted throughout the civilized world.

2. Rallying political support for the Administration at home and abroad, using this incident as a focal point.

3. Using the incident to justify the Administration's defense program and to secure the backing needed for its funding by Congress.

4. Taking such steps as would help ensure against a possible recurrence of such an incident.

By contrast, Soviet behavior permits us to derive a different set of priorities in Moscow's handling of the crisis:

1. Maintaining the regime's credibility with its primary audience and constituency—the Soviet population—and, first of all, its own elites.

2. Pursuing a strategy of damage limitation in Soviet dealings with foreign regimes and international media.

3. Seeking to deny any factual basis to the United States for its allegations concerning the Soviet role and calculus in the KAL 007 crisis.

4. Taking such steps as would help ensure against a possible recurrence of such an incident.

An appreciation of the differences between the two sets of objectives will help us to understand the differences between Moscow and Washington in the handling of events. In particular, if we recognize—as the American public was hardly invited to do at the time—the overriding priority, to the Soviet leadership, of maintaining the façade of infallibility vis-à-vis its own population and of forestalling any doubts in the minds of its own elite on whether the system worked, much in the Soviet handling of the affair becomes, if not wise or truthful, then at least intelligible.

Handling the Crisis

What to the outside world appeared as the singular ineptness in the Soviet handling of the crisis, during the initial week, must be related not only to the priority of domestic audiences, just mentioned, but also to the inherent challenge which the event presented to Soviet propagandists, as well as to the unexpectedness of the crisis. If so, this sheds an interesting light on the qualitative difference between Soviet heavy-handed improvization and carefully thought-out propaganda guidance. As we have seen, the Soviet response began with an almost infantile pretense and a determination to avoid facing the facts. The point of departure was to admit as little as possible until one knew how much information the adversary had. (In this regard, U.S. behavior after the downing of the U-2 in 1960 had not been fundamentally dissimilar.) When finally Moscow was reluctantly compelled to acknowledge that a Soviet plane had shot down the airliner, the admission sparked a media campaign marked, among other things, by continued indirection—the Soviet press avoided giving the number of victims on the plane; official statements referred to the order to "terminate the flight," not explicitly to shoot it down—and by putting the blame on the United States for an elaborate and despicable "provocation."[2] In fact, after a series of presentations of the Soviet case, by the middle of September the Soviet media turned primary attention to American subversive activities around the globe, from Nicaragua to Lebanon to Afghanistan, both to take the domestic audience's attention off the airliner case and to enshrine the Soviet version in a broader, familiar context of United States misdeeds.

From the first, primitive, "stonewalling" response, which may have served Soviet objectives at home but was clearly a public-relations disaster abroad—coupled with the unexpectedly intense, and largely negative, reaction elsewhere to the plane's destruction—the official Soviet handling became far more skilful and credible after about a week—credible, that is, within the framework of the damage already done. Under these conditions, the televised two-hour press conference by Marshal Ogarkov, flanked by Zamiatin and Kornienko, was a coup of sorts, and certainly a contrast to earlier occasions on which key actors, and especially senior military officers, had not been available to the media. Articles by key military figures and interviews with air defense officials and the pilots involved showed the unusual lengths to which Soviet propaganda now went to undo some of the harm. The Soviet public-relations effort, during the first weeks, was in large measure an effort at damage control in regard to the response abroad, primarily by means of a counterattack.

A careful analysis of Soviet press, radio, and television would permit even an outsider to reconstruct the guidance that was being issued to the Soviet media. Thus a list of questions (virtually identical in every case) kept popping up which ostensibly had not been answered by American (or Japanese, or South Korean) authorities—questions meant to incriminate the sponsors of the airliner's incursion. Then, within seventy-two hours, a battery of Soviet international law experts were trotted out to assert the legality of Soviet behavior. Some of the more ludicrous comments of the first few days vanished from the columns of the Soviet press. Moscow always likes to cite foreign comment in support of Soviet policy positions. In this instance, it had mighty little to go with, and it was obliged to fall back on a practice it has tended to shun in recent years: citing loyal communist organs abroad. Even here Moscow had to be selective, as foreign communist media were by no means unanimous or uncritical in their comments on Soviet behavior in this crisis.

As suggested above, one problem Soviet tacticians had to face—as they often do—was the need to appeal simultaneously to two distinct constituencies: a foreign audience overwhelmingly hostile to the shooting down of a civilian aircraft, and a domestic audience which needed to be impressed with the continued infallibility of the ruling party, the integrity of Soviet borders, the vigilance of its protectors, and the malice of their enemies abroad. Given the top priority of reassuring the attentive public at home, the official Soviet handling made some sense. Apparently within days, party members were being summoned to meetings to be briefed on the whole affair; according to one source, three days after the incident a confidential memorandum was sent out from Moscow to higher party organizations around the country explaining what had occurred.[3]

This did not dispose of the tension between domestic and foreign target groups: if it might have been smart vis-à-vis the outside world to admit the Soviet mishandling of the affair, it would have been unprecedented to make such a confession to one's own citizenry. Yet the difficulty went a good deal further than that: Moscow had conflicting objectives in addressing the wider audience.

> Asked why the Soviet Union did not save itself a lot of trouble by admitting that the downing had been a mistake, a senior Soviet official replied privately: "To have done so would, in effect, have legalized flights by American spy planes over our territory. Our borders would no longer be inviolate."[4]

That does indeed suggest the crux of the Soviet dilemma. It also makes more intelligible the continued contradiction in the official position, spelled out by Ogarkov and repeated endlessly since then: (1) we did not know it was a commercial plane with civilians on board; (2) if need be, we will do the same thing again.

In at least two regards, the Soviet position—though portrayed in Moscow as principled—might well have been adjudged counterproductive if the Kremlin had cared more about foreign opinion. The first relates to the Soviet refusal to pay compensation to the families of victims, as has been customary in such occurrences. Since the responsibility, according to Moscow, rests with Washington, that is where the demand for compensation should be addressed—a position rejected not only by other Western powers but also by India and China. The second is Soviet behavior in regard to the ICAO investigation. Though complying might have strengthened their case as a law-abiding member-state, the Soviet authorities failed to provide copies or transcripts of taped communications and records of radar tracking, falling back on legal arguments that under the Chicago Convention they were not obliged to do so. But, as we have seen, in the official calculus the foreign had to take second place to the domestic reaction; and falling back on a legal loophole may have spared Moscow some further embarrassment. Once again, one can only speculate whether failure to cooperate more fully with the ICAO reflected the absence of conclusive "evidence" that would have supported the Soviet case (or worse), the wish to conceal details of operational failures during the overflight, or an application of standard Soviet assertions of sovereignty vis-à-vis international law and organizations.

On balance, it might be said that the Soviet handling of the incident was reasonably successful at home and overwhelmingly a failure abroad. Given the need to choose, and given the ordering of Soviet priorities, the propaganda campaign after the first few days was probably as effective as the constraints—including the system, the events, and the mandatory ethos—allowed.*

To what extent the whole incident, and its handling afterwards, generated disagreements within the top Soviet leadership, we still do not know. We have no evidence that anyone in the elite contested the right of the military to make the decisions at the time they needed to be made: there was no reasonable alternative and no time to convene the Politburo or consult senior Party and government officials. For that matter, as was discussed elsewhere, it is by no means clear that the Politburo would have decided otherwise. If anything, it was the suggestion of inefficiency and incompetence in disposing of the "intruder" that required corrective, and perhaps punitive, action. Where there does appear to have been a good deal of unhappiness is in the handling of the disaster after it had occurred. Typically, the criticism voiced (albeit quietly) tended to be instrumental, not principled. At that stage, no doubt, the Politburo both reviewed the events and approved the guidelines for their public treatment.

There were stories in the press abroad about a split in the Soviet leadership over the whole affair, but there were bound to be such stories. They cannot be taken at face value. Certainly, the change of leadership which brought Konstantin Chernenko into the seat of Party General Secretary, upon the death of Yuri Andropov early in 1984, did not alter the public handling of the KAL 007 affair: Soviet media, civilian and military alike, continued to insist that the PVO had dealt with the matter just as it needed to be and, if the occasion arose, would do so again with due vigilance and dispatch.

---

*There is, of course, no reliable poll of Soviet public (or better, private) opinion. Some indication, in addition to dispatches by Western newspaper correspondents stationed in Moscow, may, however, be garnered in this instance from an audience and opinion research survey of some 274 Soviet travelers abroad, conducted for Radio Liberty. While there are serious questions concerning the selective of the sample, on the one hand, and the veracity of the responses, on the other, some of the findings (along with selective verbatim quotations from the interviews) appear plausible. The attitude of respondents toward the downing of the aircraft appeared to vary significantly with their major source of information. While those whose information came primarily from Soviet television and radio approved the Soviet action by better than two to one, those (relatively few) whose information came primarily from Western radio indicated a better than 50 percent disapproval. It is not clear, however, whether the latter group does not represent a preselected subset disposed to distrust Soviet news and behavior. ("The Korean Airline Incident: Western Radio and Soviet Perceptions," Radio Free Europe–Radio Liberty, Soviet Area Audience and Opinion Research, Report AR 4-84 [April 1984].)

A few things might be said, more concisely, about the official American handling of the story. The situation is of course vastly different from the Soviet scene: there is no monopoly on mass media, and there is no defensiveness over one's behavior such as characterized the Soviet posture. A good deal has become known through leaks and unattributed stories from Washington, but of course the question remains whether there is more to be discovered about the possible role of the United States (or of individual Americans) in dispatching the jet. While the Korean airliner crisis received ample space and attention, and while there has been some imaginative and determined "investigative journalism" on this subject, at least a part of the American media deserve a low grade for their failure to question government handouts and to challenge official interpretations.

This was, for all intents and purposes, the Reagan Administration's first serious confrontation with Moscow, and its response was marked by shrillness in rhetoric and passivity in behavior.[5] It is not obvious that there was an underlying rationale for this dichotomy. The verbal overkill was presumably based on a desire to capitalize politically on a rare opportunity in which Soviet "guilt" and "barbarism" were amply apparent, and to isolate Moscow, as in fact Washington was rather successful in doing—at the United Nations, at the International Civil Aviation Organization in Montreal, and in public opinion around the globe. It reflected the ongoing effort by political warfare to delegitimize the Soviet regime in the eyes of the world.

It is not clear who was the main architect of this dichotomous strategy, though it appears that the President himself had an active hand in shaping it. The Department of State saw the Korean Air Lines disaster as an opportunity to assert its own policymaking role in its rivalry with other political actors on the Washington scene, as Secretary of State George Shultz, Under Secretary Lawrence Eagleburger, and Assistant Secretary Richard Burt shaped U.S. policy.[6] To beat off attempts from other quarters—notably the Pentagon—to "get a piece of the action," the State Department responded with a verbal line unusually hard for that department. Nonetheless, when others urged a suspension of some of the arms talks with the Soviet Union, Shultz refused. It is not clear whether the failure to press for effective sanctions stemmed from earlier experiences (such as the fiasco with the Soviet natural gas pipeline in Western Europe), from a calculated desire to maintain a posture of moderation, or (less likely) from a realization that the real story was more complicated and less clear-cut than initially portrayed. One result was an exceptionally strong attack on Administration policy, not only from the political far right as too weak and "appeasing," but also from others on the American political scene. Assailing U.S. policy as a "sad mixture of jingoistic rhetoric and impotence," Dimitri Simes castigated the White House for having "said far too much and done far too little."[7]

It was elementary that the excesses in rhetoric amounted to little but grandstanding, which had some domestic and perhaps some foreign appeal but achieved nothing insofar as dealing with Moscow was concerned. As Simes put it, "there is more to a relationship with the other superpower than putting it on the defensive," and the charges and tone adopted in Washington made a less charged or more moderate response from Moscow all but impossible. Presumably, such a posture was ideologically comforting in seeming to validate some of the President's cherished (and oft-contested) assumptions about communism and the Soviet system. It did little in Moscow other than to increase the defensive combativeness of the incumbents.*

The considerable public support for the Administration's position on this issue—and the widespread demand for more energetic U.S. action in retaliation—does not appear to have been significantly affected by the somewhat embarrassing revelations, made piecemeal during the following weeks, that a number of initial U.S. allegations turned out to be wrong. Washington had erroneously insisted that the Russians knew the target was a civilian aircraft; it had denied that Soviet fighters had guns aboard which could have fired tracer shots as Moscow alleged; it had denied that the Soviet interceptor aircraft had signaled the Korean plane to land at the nearest airport; the transcript of Soviet pilot conversations had to be amended in a politically damaging way; and the presence of the RC-135 in the vicinity had initially not been revealed by Washington. All this may have raised the level of doubts in a cynical public about the U.S. handling of the whole affair, but at home and abroad the bottom line was evidently that it was a Soviet plane that had wilfully shot down the Korean aircraft.

---

*U.S. public opinion showed an exceptional receptivity to anti-Soviet themes; in fact, the Gallup Poll showed the Soviet Union at its worst ranking in American opinion since 1956. At the same time, over 60 percent of those polled in a *New York Times*/CBS poll doubted whether the U.S. government had told the full story of the Korean airliner. (*New York Times*, September 16, 1983; *Los Angeles Times*, October 24, 1983; *Newsweek*, September 19, 1983, p. 21.) There were numerous instances of communities banning the sale of Soviet vodka, and similar "linkage," as well as some ugly invasions of the Soviet residential property at Glen Cove, New York. The Federal government proved unwilling to fight New York and New Jersey when their governors refused to let Soviet foreign minister Andrei Gromyko land at any airports in their respective states to attend the United Nations General Assembly—arguably, a violation of U.S. treaty commitments—because the White House did not want to appear easier on the Russians than the two governors. (*New York Times*, September 19 and 22, 1983.)

Crisis Management and Learning

How was the crisis engendered by the flight of KAL 007 managed by the two superpowers? For Moscow, the whole concept of crisis management is a strange and unfamiliar one. During the crisis, Soviet priorities and thinking went in other directions: how to persuade their own population and their allies and friends of the wisdom of their own behavior, how to minimize the political costs to themselves, how to improve their position relative to the United States, and—for the leaders exposed by the events—how to protect their political backsides. We have seen the impact of collective memories, of bureaucratic behavior, of military reflexes, of institutional arrangements such as the compartmentalization and censorship of information, of incompetence, and of the pervasive sense of insecurity which time and again has given rise, on the Soviet side, to a troublesome pattern of pre-emptive nervousness.[8]

For Washington, as we saw, the concern seemed to be one of scoring points, exposing the adversary, being proven right, using the crisis for political gains. The media, with frequent references to "murder in cold blood," "ambush," "massacre," and equivalent phrases, contributed to the rhetorical excess that masked the lack of sanctions against Moscow. But after the first few days of confused verbal escalation, a decision was taken—apparently at the level of the National Security Council—not to invite an all-out confrontation with the Soviet Union over this issue. As the President remarked (forgetting the newly signed grain deal), to any sanctions the U.S. took—such as recalling its ambassador—Moscow could reciprocate in kind. This implied managing the crisis so as not to let it escalate any further—in other words, not tying the matter at hand in habitual "linkage" to other issues such as technology transfer or arms-control talks. While this set the formal limits to the crisis, at least in American intent, in fact the impact of the events went well beyond the airliner and its casualties. By reversing the mood and aggravating the climate of relations, it first stalled and then doomed other Soviet-American dealings as well.

One circumstance which made it more difficult to deal with the crisis at hand and which contributed to the negative effect of the crisis on Soviet-American relations was the virtual incompatibility of the Soviet and American versions of the events. In this regard, it continued a dangerous tendency of the two superpowers to produce, to follow—and to believe—two vastly different scripts. As Alexander George has noted, especially since the Soviet invasion of Afghanistan each side has succumbed to the temptation of developing its own self-serving account—all the more dangerous because sincerely believed—of why the détente relationship has eroded. As a result, U.S. and Soviet leaders are now operating with sharply conflicting explanations for what went wrong and who is to blame.... Instruments of self-justification and assertions of blame are steadily hardening.... This inflexibility is leading inexorably to a new group of rigid mind-sets and mutually hostile images that will severely constrain efforts to halt the drift into a new version of the cold war.[9]

While Moscow—as we have seen earlier—surely has been capable of brazenly insisting on would-be facts which are demonstrably not so, the above statement correctly points to the important fact that the Soviet authorities possess not only the capacity to unleash a propaganda barrage whose themes bear little resemblance to reality (as, at times, do other regimes) but also quite frequently the disposition to believe what they say. All too often their arguments are congruent with the mind-set and the broader assumptions that describe their world-view. This of course makes finding a common language significantly more difficult, in and out of crisis situations.

Did either side learn from the crisis? For Moscow, the flight of KAL 007 revealed once more and all too dramatically the penetrability—not to say the porousness—of its air defenses in the Far East. It showed how both technical imperfection and human errors had contributed to the crisis—to begin with, by failing to identify the intruder-plane; and no doubt an early decision after the crisis was over must have been to work on improving both the technical and the human dimension. A shake-up of personnel in the Far Eastern air defense command was in fact reported about one month later.[10] It is safe to assert that it reflected unhappiness with the way the PVO had functioned during the crisis—not unhappiness with shooting down the jet but, on the contrary, with failing to respond more promptly, vigorously, and effectively.[11]

There is no reason to think that the incident led Moscow to reconsider the delegation of limited decision-making to the various air-defense theaters around the country; nor is there any reason to link (as some Western comments have) such trigger-happiness as the destruction of the Korean jet revealed to the potential use of nuclear weapons, control over which appears to have been and to have remained centrally and carefully secured.

Several articles in Soviet military publications, since the incident, have used it to illustrate the need for better training and preparedness of Soviet air defense personnel, including the need for fighter pilots to correctly identify strange aircraft, if necessary to force them to land, and in any case to make the final decisions by themselves. The Soviets have recognized past shortcomings in training and performance and have stressed the need for greater individual responsibility.[12]

An American magazine has reported that since the incident "U.S. commanders have detected a major buildup of Soviet antiaircraft facilities in the Far East. The Soviets are also keeping a much closer watch over U.S. reconnaissance flights in the region. In the past the tracking of U.S. RC-135s was a lazy ritual; now the Russians send up several planes to tail every U.S. spy plane."[13] Reportedly there were at least two Soviet simulations of the KAL intrusion, presumably as training exercises, in 1984. All published Soviet accounts have continued to justify and praise the behavior of the ground controllers and fighter pilots who brought KAL 007 down.[14]

What, if anything, the United States learned from the crisis remains to be seen. The lingering doubts about the U.S. role in what happened are bound to persist. What the disaster is likely to have brought home to many observers is hardly a novel insight: the reality of Soviet-American relations is serious enough, and the international balance is fragile enough, under the best of conditions, not to be burdened with additional emotional and unforeseen confrontations. The overlay of perceptual problems, of misconceptions which are deeply embedded in the world-view of each side, and the tendency to overreact under crisis conditions render these relations that much more difficult to manage.

Short of bringing about a general improvement in relations, what can be done to reduce the chances of other such crises occurring in the future and to reduce the dangers if they do occur? There are the short-term tasks, some of which are beginning to be addressed: improvements in the mechanics and rules of communication among aircraft and ground traffic stations, between civilian and military ground controllers, in radar identification, and the like.

The ICAO, whose Council on March 6, 1984 accepted (by a vote of twenty to two—the two being the Soviet Union and Czechoslovakia—with nine abstentions) the staff report condemning Soviet behavior in shooting down KAL 007, has begun to address some of these questions, and apparently Soviet representatives have shown an interest in such technical—though, of course, not political—improvements. In early May 1984, the ICAO Assembly, after a three-week session, unanimously adopted an amendment to the 1944 Chicago Convention which includes a ban on the use of weapons against civilian aircraft, and in a separate resolution called for improved coordination between military and civil communications systems and air traffic control agencies.[15]

The absence of so-called back channels—i.e., private, unadvertised contacts outside the official diplomatic process—to communicate with their opposite numbers in the Soviet Union (a technique frequently employed during the preceding generation) deprived the White House of opportunities to exchange messages informally, frankly, and out of public sight. Especially at times when tensions and blood pressure mount on both sides, this meant foregoing a possibly useful device—useful if, and only if, there had been a desire to forego public grandstanding and to eschew capitalizing politically on the Soviet deed. But this was not the case.

Theoretically, if there had been an effective code of conduct, or rules of the game, to which both superpowers adhered—not only in principle but in fact, dealing not only with pious generalities but with practical specifics—it might have been possible to promptly initiate a joint (or a third-party) investigation, with both sides withholding charges beyond a simple recital of events until a report (or, failing a single report, separate reports by the investigating parties) was produced. In actuality, given the nature of Soviet-American relations and the political climate in each of the countries concerned, such a scheme would have been wildly unrealistic (even if Moscow had recognized the legitimacy of an American interest in the whole affair, which it did not). In fact, neither side made any proposal that would have moved in this direction.

The high cost of error under conditions of hair-trigger security need scarcely be dramatized. But in the long run, there remain the more difficult tasks of correcting mutual misconceptions and working toward a more stable security environment in which events such as those discussed here, if they cannot be prevented altogether, need not become international crises.

We have discussed the weight of relatively enduring factors such as mind-sets and bureaucratic politics in explaining the behavior of the two superpowers. What about the role of the political context, at home and especially abroad? For instance, would the outcome have been the same if the incident had taken place in 1973, at the height of Soviet-American détente? The answer is bound to be speculative, but it is not clear that the decision on the Soviet side would have been fundamentally different. Assuming that it would also have been taken by the military without direct reference to top-level civilian authorities, the decision might well have been the same. In the 1978 incident involving another South Korean airliner—something of a relevant precedent—the Soviet authorities clearly decided that the jet had to be forced to land, if need be by shooting it down, but preferably without utter destruction. On the other hand, the earlier experience suggests that the aftermath of the incident would in all likelihood have been handled far more smoothly, less dramatically, and less precipitously. Thus the relative importance of the political context—notably the state of Soviet-American relations—cannot be adequately tested in comparable situations and remains a variable of uncertain weight.

Soviet-American relations also went into a tailspin as a consequence of the crisis over KAL 007. While, by the end of September 1983, given the characteristically short attention span of U.S. media and public discourse, American officials began to shift away from the extreme rhetoric that had marked the initial American reaction, the Soviet response, on the contrary, hardened after a few weeks. After having been silent— reportedly on vacation away from Moscow and, as it now appears, seriously ill—Yuri Andropov resurfaced, if not in person, then in name. A statement attributed to him was officially released in Moscow on September 28. It strongly suggested that the smoldering dispute over the question whether the Soviet Union could get along with the Reagan Administration had been resolved in the negative, and the airliner episode had figured in the argument. Andropov declared:

> Even if someone had illusions as to the possible evolution for the better in the policy of the present American Administration, the latest developments have dispelled them. For the sake of its imperial ambitions it is going so far that one begins to doubt whether it has any brakes preventing it from crossing the mark before which any sober-minded person would stop.
>
> The sophisticated provocation masterminded by the United States special services with the use of a South Korean plane is an example of extreme adventurism in politics. We have elucidated the factual aspect of the action thoroughly and authentically. The guilt of its organizers, no matter how hard they may dodge and what false versions they may put forward, has been proved.
>
> The Soviet leadership expressed regret over the loss of human life resulting from that unprecedented, criminal subversion. It is on the conscience of those who would like to assume the right not to reckon with the sovereignty of states and the inviolability of borders, who masterminded and carried out the provocation, who literally on the following day hastily pushed through Congress colossal military spending and are now rubbing their hands with pleasure.[16]

Whether or not in the absence of this incident an improvement in superpower relations could have come about, and perhaps an agreement reached that would have forestalled the deployment of new NATO missiles, remains a matter of speculation. A good case can be made that under no circumstances was a significant improvement of relations in the cards.[17] But even if that was the case, the result was that in Washington (as one correspondent reported) officials now "saw little likelihood of any productive discussions until after the 1984 elections," while in Moscow "the incident is going to affect East-West relations here for a long time to come, mainly because of the way the Soviets are handling it," said one Western ambassador there. "They're giving us nothing with which we could argue for a change in the U.S. approach to the problem."[18] Moreover, an unadvertised consequence of the incident was, first, to weaken and paralyze the bureaucratic coalition in Washington which, on the eve of the downing of KAL 007, had been prepared to explore improved Soviet-American relations, and, in turn, to strengthen the diehards at the White House, the Pentagon, and the U.S. mission to the UN.

In the year following the crisis, Soviet-American relations were in as bad a shape as they had been for a generation or more, and on both sides the memory of the airliner disaster lingered on. Indeed, the first anniversary of the KAL disaster precipitated a new Soviet media campaign on the subject, remarkable for several things: it included arguments and dispatches even more primitive than the previous year's treatment; it relied entirely on news reports from non-Soviet sources; and its thrust was not so much to make the Soviet version of events credible as to underscore and illustrate the ostensibly pernicious nature of the Reagan regime.[19]

Route R20 was temporarily closed down to civil aviation as too risky to fly. Korean Air Lines did not win any international awards for its performance record. It continued to fly its regular routes, but at least for some time with a larger proportion of empty seats. Under a new management, it offered some $100,000 in compensation and so-called condolence money to the families of each victim of flight 007, something which some of the families welcomed and which others rejected as insulting.[20] Numerous lawsuits were lodged by families of survivors—against KAL, the U.S. government, and a variety of other targets, making sure that the affair would remain in the public eye. Conspiracy buffs continued to comb the debris of information for new clues and hypotheses that would explain it all. Meanwhile, the KAL flight from New York to Seoul was redesignated flight 017: there is no more KAL 007.

Perceptions and Politics

Of all the incidents between East and West since World War II, the downing of KAL 007 was the disaster most costly in human lives. The fate of the unfortunate airliner highlights the volatility of the international order. An unforeseen incident or accident, a single plane or a single person—and *a fortiori* a single nuclear device—can create an international crisis of the first order, whatever the intentions of the so-called policymakers. And once an incident occurs, each side sees itself compelled to respond—to speak out or to act—and to do so fast and firmly, as if it knew what it was all about. The dangers that inhere in such a pattern of behavior are only too obvious, yet so are the pressures that bring it about.

The flight of KAL 007 challenged a number of beliefs and illusions. Some of these stem from our general faith in science and technology. Thus, there has been widespread acceptance of the notion that a variety of technological innovations—radar, satellite photography, electronic communications networks, sonar detection—have made deterrence of aggression and intrusion, nuclear as well as conventional, more reliable and therefore stable, and have made unilateral verification of arms-limitation agreements more foolproof and violations less likely because of the greater probability of detection. The opponents of arms-control agreements have likewise invoked the reliability of weapons technology (say, in the ability to "launch on warning") as part of the argument that security is better assured by technical than by political means.

The crisis over KAL 007 does not disprove these arguments; but it does underscore not only the limits of technology but in particular the hazards of inadequate technology (such as Soviet radar that could not tell that a Boeing 747 was not an RC-135; or the inability of air traffic ground controllers to check independently on the accuracy of pilots' position reports; and perhaps the malfunctions, if there were any, on board KAL 007). It bodes ill for the enthusiasts of "star wars" in the uncertain future. But, more immediately, it also illustrates how, regardless of science and technology, it is ultimately human judgments, human choices, human errors, politics, and preconceptions that shape political and military decisions.

To many American military analysts, the unreliability of Soviet early-warning systems is troublesome—especially at a time when Pershing-2's are being deployed in Europe. Yet in the end, it was not the inadequacy of Soviet technology, such as the communications link between Sakhalin and Moscow, that was the problem in the Korean airliner crisis, but the choices which the key actors made, such as the decision to shoot down the jet rather than to let it "escape" scot-free. Whether the failure of the airliner to respond to the signals from Soviet fighters and ground stations was a matter of human choice or technology is, of course, one of the questions to which we lack a definitive answer. In fact, one may speculate that greater human ingenuity might have permitted KAL 007 to "escape" even when the Soviet interceptors were in hot pursuit during its final minutes over Sakhalin, had it acknowledged their signals and feigned compliance while changing altitude and speed to get away over international waters.

Still, the lessons Moscow is apt to have drawn from the incident are likely to have borne in both directions—training as well as technology. In the latter group, while Moscow obviously knew of the extensive American effort to intercept and decode Soviet communications, it is possible that the revelations by the American and Japanese authorities brought home to the Soviet political leadership its vulnerability to foreign "ears" listening in—an unwitting Soviet exposure, a nakedness (as Soviet officials have at times referred to it), ranging apparently from missile test telemetry to perhaps civil and military communications across the country. One prompt response was reportedly a change of codes and radio frequencies on Soviet military aircraft transmissions, within literally a few days of the Japanese and American disclosure of the intercepts.[21] How extensive such changes have been cannot be judged by those outside the area of classified information.

Both sides to a dispute—both sides in a crisis—feel compelled to make decisions under conditions of imperfect information.[22] Under such conditions, each party, in its attempt to interpret such facts as are available, to fit them into some explanatory or conceptual framework, and to move toward some action strategy, inevitably tends to fall back on prior images, assumptions, and suspicions regarding the adversary power and its intentions and capabilities—images and assumptions that must have been close to the surface but come into the open only under such special circumstances. And when—as in this case—the events are such as to permit both sides to impute the worst to, and believe the worst about, the adversary, there is indeed a strong predisposition to go for "worst-case" scenarios, that is, to select from the whole range of possible interpretations the one which assumes the worst about the other side's intentions and capabilities—a tendency which, more often than not, has an inherent propensity toward self-fulfilling prophecy.

Most striking in the case we have just examined was the mind-set—the set of assumptions and beliefs dominant from the outset in official circles both in Moscow and in Washington. In their eagerness to make political capital and to impute criminal intent to their adversary, the policymakers in both the United States and the Soviet Union ruled out categories such as accident, confusion, incompetence, or error on the part of the other side as a possible explanation for the events. For Moscow to make such a defense of its behavior would have meant to admit fault and imperfection. For

Washington so to brand Soviet behavior would have blunted the ideological edge of its outrage. As a result, each side was programmed to present the whole episode as more calculated by the adversary and more overdetermined by the totality of "objective" and "subjective" forces than was warranted by the facts. Thus they revealed instead a natural predisposition to impute purpose—hostile intent, subversion, or wilful brutality—to the adversary: a dangerous but rather characteristic practice.[23]

In fact, this tendency was not limited to government analysts but included Soviet PVO radar technicians, pilots, and ground controllers: operating in an atmosphere of perennial "dueling" with the Americans, the question whether what they "saw" was conceivably a commercial plane with civilian passengers, and whether the aircraft might have made an error in navigation, does not seem to have been seriously explored by the Soviet air defense personnel. The built-in bias under such conditions is to avoid alternatives that make one appear weak, soft, or naive. Hence the tendency never to give the adversary the benefit of the doubt: in neither system is one likely to be punished for playing it tough and "going by the book."

This pervasive tendency is further strengthened by a peculiar nuclear anticipation that has developed over the past generation: the Soviet fighter pilots interviewed on television, some two weeks later, spoke (quite characteristically) not only of the broader pattern of American mischief into which the intruder-plane's action seemed to fit but also of the belief that, if indeed this plane's flight was in some respects an unprecedented phenomenon, this might be all the more dangerous. After all, who knows whether it might not be carrying a bomb or some nuclear device?

Nor was the American perception much more balanced or cautious. Why and how KAL 007 wound up where it did does not seem to have intrigued those analyzing the events when the news of the disaster first came in. How the Soviet authorities were bound to have seen it was irrelevant. That Soviet air defense personnel might have tried to signal it or get it to land was apparently ruled out as incongruent with the explanatory syndrome of inhumanity and purposive brutality. Instead, purpose, conspiracy, and provocation became the dominant assumptions on both sides. And on the American side, too, that image of evildoing was promptly fitted into a broader canvas that ranged from Afghanistan to forced labor, and soon (as in President Reagan's and Ambassador Kirkpatrick's speeches) the shooting down of the airliner came to be seen as an instance of natural, almost inevitable behavior for a totalitarian regime whose assessment this Administration saw dramatically validated by this crisis.

The crisis over the downing of KAL 007 thus served as a sort of political Rorschach test which made manifest each elite's propensities, and especially its fears and images of the adversary. Alas, the images on both sides were seriously wide of the mark. If the Soviet image of the United States was close to a caricature, the American image of the Soviet Union—both among government spokespersons and in the media— revealed an amazing lack of knowledge, feel, and understanding of the Soviet scene. To point to only one widespread misconception: in a real sense, the episode teaches us nothing about Soviet foreign-policy decisions, for shooting down the airliner was not an act implementing a foreign-policy decision of the Kremlin's leadership. Contrary to many pundits, it did not mark the beginning of a new policy. Yet one inevitable outcome of the crisis was to heighten mutual suspicion and to insulate even further each side's perceptions and rhetoric from critical testing by interaction with the other side.

In the end, however, the symmetry between the two sides breaks down. Though we have some good surmises, we do not know why KAL 007 went astray. We do know who shot it down. Politically and morally, the whole episode amounted to an international fiasco for the Soviet Union, whose leaders—once the crisis occurred—could not see any ready way out of the difficulties, which they were loath to acknowledge. Still, the United States, too, emerged from the crisis paradoxically confused— seemingly "victorious" though uncertain just what it had won, feeling morally united and superior but also conscious of serious unanswered questions and gnawing doubts.

Political scientists may, of course, argue that what we have dealt with here was not properly a war-threatening international crisis. For one thing, if we take a widely accepted definition, such a crisis requires surprise, a high level of threat, and a short decision time.[24] While the element of surprise was present in this case, there was no high threat; and the short decision time, on the American side, was self-imposed. The circumstance that it was not a war-threatening crisis (such as the Cuban missile crisis had been) but rather what has been called a "politically-damaging crisis" (as had also been true, for instance, of the U-2 incident in 1960 and of the discovery of the so-called Soviet brigade in Cuba in 1980) made it easier for the U.S. not to escalate without losing face—especially as it was by no means clear what escalation could have achieved.

For another thing, if we take the standard view that war-threatening crises are essentially bargaining situations[25] or occasions for what has been labeled "coercive diplomacy,"[26] the KAL 007 episode again does not fit the mould. The incident was hardly planned to create a negotiating situation. The Soviet Union was not trying to coerce the United States to admit its responsibility for the flight; nor, in fact, was the U.S. trying to coerce the USSR: rather it was trying to "expose" and pillory it and perhaps hoping to punish it. As in other instances, anti-Soviet sanctions were adopted more as tokens of outrage and solidarity (or, others would say, as U.S.-inspired propaganda gestures) than as credible efforts to get Moscow to admit its responsibility, to provide compensation to the families of the victims, and to learn the proper lessons from the events.

Actually, as we have seen, when it comes to learning lessons, in all likelihood the two superpowers agreed only on the most limited, technical lessons (such as the need for better civil-military air traffic communications). Beyond that, rather than bringing them closer together, what each side learned from the incident—over the outrage, both genuine and sham, directed at each other—served to place them even farther apart. In the absence of the real "black box" from KAL 007, each side filled its mental, imaginary black box with opposite and incompatible assumptions about the adversary—assumptions which, each believed, were validated by the so-called facts in the case.

Notes

Chapter 1

1. *New York Times,* September 1, 1983. (Hereinafter, unless otherwise indicated, all dates given in notes will be assumed to refer to 1983.)

2. Federal Broadcasting Information Service, *Daily Report: USSR* (hereinafter cited as *FBIS:USSR*), September 1, p. Cl.

3. Ibid., pp. C1-2 (Tokyo radio in English, 1348 GMT, September 1). Japanese involvement was presumably due in part to the presence of twenty-eight Japanese passengers on the plane. The plane carried a total crew of twenty-nine and 240 passengers, including (according to KAL) seventy-five Korean nationals, sixty-six United States citizens, twenty-eight Japanese, a number of Taiwanese, Filipinos, Chinese from Hong Kong, and Canadians, as well as nationals of at least six other countries. South Korea has no diplomatic relations with the Soviet Union. The Americans aboard included Congressman Larry P. McDonald, Democrat of Georgia, the national chairman of the John Birch Society.

4. *Pravda,* September 2, p. 5; *New York Times,* September 2; *FBIS:USSR,* September 1, p. C2. The text is the official Soviet English-language version, with corrections from the Russian original supplied in brackets.

5. *New York Times,* September 2; *Newsweek,* September 12.

6. On Soviet-American relations, see, e.g., John Lewis Gaddis, "The Rise, Fall, and Future of Detente," *Foreign Affairs,* Winter 1983/84; Alexander George, ed., *Managing U.S.-Soviet Rivalry* (Boulder, Colo.: Westview Press, 1983); Alexander Dallin and Gail W. Lapidus, "Reagan and the Russians," in Kenneth Oye et al., eds., *Eagle Defiant* (Boston: Little, Brown, 1983).

7. See Hedrick Smith, "U.S. Officials See Less Strain in Soviet Ties," *New York Times,* August 9; and Bernard Gwertzman, "U.S. and Russians to Seek New Pacts," *New York Times,* August 27.

8. *New York Times,* September 2; and *Newsweek,* September 12. Pavlov, the Soviet ambassador to Japan, in communicating the official Soviet version to the Foreign Ministry in Tokyo, even after Secretary Shultz's report that KAL 007 had been destroyed by a missile fired from a Soviet fighter, reportedly insisted (as his instructions no doubt required) that the intruding plane had left Soviet airspace and that the Soviet Union had found signs of an aircraft crash west of Moneron Island. (Radio Tokyo in English, 0146 GMT, September 2.)

9. *Pravda,* September 3; *Current Digest of the Soviet Press* [hereinafter cited as *CDSP*], Vol. XXXV, no. 35, pp. 1–2. The statement was accompanied by a map showing the inter-

national air route from Anchorage to Seoul and the course ostensibly taken by the "intruder-plane." During the following days, the Soviet press, television, and radio stepped up their counterattack in clearly coordinated fashion, charging U.S. responsibility for sending KAL 007 on an intelligence mission over sensitive Soviet installations. See, e.g., the articles by V. Zakharov in *Pravda*, September 7; by O. Piliugin in *Krasnaia Zvezda*, September 7; and by Aleksandr Bovin in *Izvestiia*, September 8.

10. *New York Times*, September 4.

11. Ibid., September 5 and 6. It was not revealed when the President and the Secretary of State were first informed of the presence of the RC-135 in the area. Washington took pains to depict the RC-135 mission as routine and as limited to a "figure 8" over international waters off the Soviet coast. It did not say whether other RC-135s went up.

12. *Pravda*, September 5; *FBIS: USSR*, September 6, p. C9; *CDSP*, Vol. XXXV, no. 35, pp. 4–5. See also Vitalii Korionov, "Politika diversii protiv mira," *Pravda*, September 6; *Literaturnaia gazeta*, September 7; *FBIS: USSR*, September 7, pp. C6–9.

13. Rowland Evans and Robert Novak, "A Missed Chance?" *Washington Post*, September 9. See also note 23, below.

14. "President Reagan: Korean Airline Massacre," U.S. Department of State, Bureau of Public Affairs, *Current Policy*, no. 507 (September 5, 1983).

15. United Nations, Security Council, *Provisional Verbatim Record*, September 6, 1983, Doc. S/PV.2471, pp. 2–20; see also *New York Times*, September 7. For one discussion of the UN politics involved, see Richard Rohmer, *Massacre 747* (Markham, Ont., Canada: PaperJacks, 1984), pp. 165–75. For a good selection of relevant United Nations documents, see American Society of International Law, *International Legal Materials*, 1983, pp. 1109–48. The same issue also includes subsequent diplomatic notes and relevant ICAO documentation.

16. The translation provided here follows *CDSP*, Vol. XXXV, no. 35, pp. 9–10; see also *Pravda*, September 7; *New York Times*, September 7; and UN, *Record*, September 6, 1983, Doc. S/PV.2472.

17. UN, *Record*, September 12, 1983, Doc. S/PV.2476, pp. 53–55; *New York Times*, September 13.

The 33-member Council of the International Civil Aviation Organization (ICAO) met in special session in Montreal on September 15, and the following day adopted (by 26 to 2) a resolution substantially similar to the Security Council's (in a body where the Soviet Union possessed no veto power), including the call for an international investigation, over Soviet objections. On the deliberations of the ICAO Executive Committee, see ICAO Document 9409, A24-EX, *Executive Committee: Report and Minutes* (September–October 1983).

The 38th session of the UN General Assembly opened on September 20 with Soviet Foreign Minister Andrei Gromyko absent, for the first time in many years, after the governors of New York and New Jersey had refused to let the Soviet plane carrying him land either at John F. Kennedy or at Newark Airport. They made clear that their action was in retaliation for the Soviet downing of the Korean airliner. Although the State Department had offered to let Gromyko land on a military airfield (provided he arrived in a military plane, since Aeroflot aircraft were banned), Moscow charged the U.S. with violating its obligations to assure normal conditions of access, as required by international agreement.

18. On September 6, Under Secretary of State Lawrence S. Eagleburger issued a "toughly worded" statement regarding the Soviet admission of responsibility for downing the South Korean jetliner, stressing that several particulars in the Soviet government statement were ostensibly "not borne out by the facts." Instead of "lies and half-truths," it demanded a full accounting, a Soviet apology, compensation for the victims' families, and Soviet cooperation in an international investigation. (See *New York Times*, September 7.)

On September 8, Secretary of State George P. Shultz had a meeting with Soviet Foreign Minister Gromyko in Madrid, where both officials were expected to take part in the concluding sessions of the protracted Conference on Security and Cooperation in Europe. By all accounts, Shultz confronted Gromyko in a stiff and sharp manner, renewing the American charges, and was in turn treated to a Soviet rebuttal which repeated Soviet allegations blaming the United States, explanations which, later on, Shultz declared to have been "totally unacceptable." (*New York Times*, September 8 and 9.)

19. For the Ogarkov press conference, see the transcript of the television transmission,

Moscow Intervision in Russian, in *FBIS:USSR*, September 12, 1983, pp. DD10–31, and September 19, p. DD21. For published TASS versions, see *New York Times*, September 10; *Pravda*, September 10; *CDSP*, Vol. XXXV, no. 36, pp. 1–5. See also *FBIS:USSR*, September 9, pp. DD1–3; September 12, pp. DD1–9; and September 13, pp. DD3–7.

20. See *New York Times*, September 11; *Krasnaia Zvezda*, September 13; *CDSP*, Vol. XXXV, no. 37, pp. 7–9; *FBIS:USSR*, September 12, pp. DD32–41, and September 23, pp. DD1–2.

21. Marshal P. Kirsanov, "Fakty izoblichaiut Vashington," *Pravda*, September 20; *New York Times*, September 20; *CDSP*, Vol. XXXV, no. 38, pp. 6–7.

22. Similarly, the Soviet Union had insisted that the Su-15 had a radio transmitter operating on the standard international search and rescue frequency of 121.5 MHz, which had been used to contact KAL 007; ostensibly it had not replied. The United States had argued that Soviet planes had no such capability, and various officials, from the President to Korean Air Lines' officials, "explained" that Moscow would not let Soviet pilots use such an emergency frequency out of fear of their defection, since it would permit them to communicate with ground controllers (and pilots) on the other side. Whether or not many Soviet PVO fighters had such equipment, at least some Su-15s had them, it turned out, as Soviet officials were eager to demonstrate to the satisfaction of a visiting team from the ICAO later in the year. According to Rohmer (*Massacre 747*, p. 183), Major General George Keegan, former U.S. Air Force Chief of Intelligence, likewise stated that the Su-15 was equipped to use the 121.5 frequency. On the other hand, the ICAO staff remained skeptical, the report of its Air Navigation Commission concluding that there is no evidence "of any calls on 121.5 MHz having been heard by any civil or military ground unit or by other aircraft within VHF range of the intercepting aircraft." (ICAO, Air Navigation Commission, Document C-WP/7809, February 16, 1984, p. 9.)

23. *New York Times*, September 11, 18, and 21. In an interview with *TIME* correspondent Laurence I. Barrett, Reagan remarked (*TIME*, September 19, p. 21):

> A.—Obviously you are tempted to think about vengeance, but there is no way you can avenge such a thing.... But what you have to look for is what you can do, first of all, to get restitution for the families of the victims, and what you can do to see that this never happens again.
>
> Q.—That's your answer to those who say you should have acted in much tougher fashion?
>
> A.—Yes, I've noticed that many of the people sounding off at great length now, being very vocal about this, in many instances they don't suggest what [specific] things I could do. [Or] they suggest things that are so obvious that they were the first things we thought of and ruled out for equally obvious reasons.
>
> Q.—Such as canceling the newly signed grain agreement?
>
> A.—Yes....There were a number of other things that show your displeasure, but they could respond with retaliation of the same kind.
>
> Q.—You never seriously considered suspending INF and START?
>
> A.—No.

24. For copies of pre-flight operational data and maintenance in Anchorage, see ICAO, *Final Report of Investigation* (Doc. C-WP/7764), December 2, 1983 (hereinafter cited as *ICAO Report*), Appendix A. For information on the flight crew and the condition of the aircraft, see Republic of Korea, Incident Investigation Committee, *Interim Report on Incident Investigation*, September 1983, in Appendix G, pp. 6 ff.

25. For the record of flight times and fuel consumption during July and August 1983, see *ICAO Report*, Appendix G, pp. 21–25. For a transcription of Anchorage/Tower communications with KE007 before and after takeoff, see ibid., Appendix C, "Air-Ground Communications," pp. 1–2. (KE007 is the abbreviated notation for Korean Air Lines 007 used in the international civil aviation system.)

26. *ICAO Report*, p. 5. These and subsequent data are taken from the *ICAO Report* and its Appendix C, the transcription of recorded air-ground communications.

Prior to 1976, Anchorage-Tokyo air traffic operated essentially on random routes as far north as possible to avoid strong winds in this area. As air traffic increased, a three-route system was introduced and in 1980 expanded to five parallel routes with not less than fifty-mile lateral separation and 1,000-feet vertical separation between any two. R20 and R80 were used for westbound flights, A90, R91, and G44 for eastbound flights.

27. Ibid., Appendix C, pp. C9–10; *Washington Post,* September 17; Tokyo NHK Television, September 16, trans. in *FBIS:Japan,* September 19, pp. C2–3.

28. *ICAO Report,* Appendix F, pp. F3, F11; Ogarkov press conference, *Pravda,* September 10.

29. *ICAO Report,* Appendix F, pp. F3, F11. See also David Shribman, "Korean Jetliner: What Is Known and What Isn't," *New York Times,* September 8, and "The Last Hours of Flight 007," *New York Times,* September 26.

30. Ambassador Kirkpatrick, at UN Security Council, in UN, *Record.*

31. The recording continues until 1846:09 hours. See *New York Times,* September 7; UN Security Council, *Provisional Verbatim Record,* September 6, Doc. S/PV.2471, pp. 6–10; *Aviation Week and Space Technology,* September 12, pp. 22–23, and September 19; *ICAO Report,* Appendix D, pp. D1–3. As reproduced above, the text has been slightly corrected on the basis of the Russian-language originals. The following are additional excerpts from the same tape, after the shooting down of the 747:

1826:53	DEP	805	Fuel remainder 1,600.
1827:01	DEP	805	Am executing. What is the distance to the airfield?
1827:05	DEP	805	Roger.
1828:05	DEP	805	[In response to query from *Deputat* whether he launched one or two missiles] I launched both.
1829:05	DEP	163	What is the distance to the target?
1829:13	DEP	163	No, I don't see it. . . .
1832:12	DEP	163	Executing [course] 210.
1832:22	DEP	163	What is the target's altitude? [My] course is 210.
1832:41	DEP	163	What is the distance to the target? . . . Roger. Me too. . . . What am I to do now?
1835:54	TRI	121	Do you see the target?
	TRI	121	No, I don't see [it].
1836:02	DEP	121	He doesn't see the target.

From both Japanese and American sources, there were initially clear indications that not only air-to-ground but also ground-to-air communications had been intercepted. In fact, Kyodo in Tokyo on September 1 released several excerpts including exchanges such as "Take aim at the target." "Aim taken." According to another report, after the missiles were fired, there was this exchange:

Unidentified questioner: "Where did it go?"

Reply: "We shot it down."

Government spokesman Masaharu Gotoda declared on September 6 that "Japan has also monitored communication from the ground to the fighter but will not release it." The existence of such intercepts was promptly denied by Defense Vice Minister Haruo Natsume. (*FBIS:Japan,* September 2, p. C1; September 6, pp. C4–6; September 7, pp. C1–2; September 12, p. C1; *TIME,* September 12, p. 15.)

It is known that the Japanese Defense Agency has "a voice-activated recording machine going at all times, monitoring every frequency used by the Soviets in controlling their fighters." According to one account, the Japanese monitored three sets of two-way conversations between Soviet ground control and fighter pilots. (Rohmer, *Massacre 747,* pp. 125, 129 ff.)

Larry Speakes, the White House spokesman, first indicated that the U.S. had clear evidence that the Soviet authorities knew they ordered a civilian plane shot down and that the order had come from ground control stations, but then reversed himself, saying that releasing such information would compromise U.S. intelligence activities. After earlier indicating that the U.S. had tapes of ground-to-air transmissions, on September 7 he denied that the U.S. had any. (See *New York Times,* September 8.) According to Anthony Sampson: "The United States reneged on a pledge to Japan to reveal its two-hour radio transcripts of Flight 007 after the Japanese made public their record of the plane's last fifteen minutes. The U.S. thus embarrassed the Japanese, along with exposing their monitoring capability." ("What Happened to Flight 007?" *Parade Magazine,* April 22, 1984, p. 12.)

Although it is widely assumed that the United States government attempts to monitor Soviet communications, Washington has rather consistently denied the existence of such intercepts in American hands, perhaps for reasons of diplomatic propriety, more likely to minimize the chances of the Soviet authorities beginning to encrypt more of their domestic transmissions. An apparently authoritative account spoke of the systematic U.S. monitoring of Soviet radar signals from ground installations and aircraft in the Far East, until recently collected and translated in Japan or Okinawa. "Now a new satellite permits the flow of raw data in 'real time'—almost instantaneously—to NSA headquarters at Ft. Meade, Md. Still, the Japanese continue to monitor, translate and analyze Soviet transmissions on their own, from an isolated complex of white geodesic domes at the Wakkanai base.... As to whether Shultz [and later Kirkpatrick] revealed too much [in their statements on the Korean jet incident], some intelligence veterans agreed that such disclosures always made them nervous.... What Shultz is not likely to reveal is the top-secret intelligence that other U.S. systems may have gathered [on the same attack].... But experts said that the Soviets' increased use of modern microwave links for their confidential telephone conversations in recent years had made them more vulnerable than ever to the spy satellites, surveillance planes, electronic listening posts and computer-assisted code breakers of the eavesdroppers at NSA." (*Newsweek,* September 12, p. 25. See also *Aviation Week and Space Technology,* September 12, pp. 19–20.)

32. *New York Times,* September 13. American specialists concluded that the Su-15 had employed infrared guided missiles with a 70-lb. high-explosive warhead, probably homed on the engines on one of the plane's wings. (Clarence A. Robinson, Jr., "U.S. Says Soviets Knew Korean Air Lines 747 Was Commercial Flight," *Aviation Week and Space Technology,* September 12, p. 21.) While most observers have accepted this account of a ten- or twelve-minute span from the time the airliner was hit until it disappeared from Japanese and Soviet radar screens, Canadian Major General (ret.) Richard Rohmer challenges this notion. According to him, one missile was heat-seeking, the other radar-controlled and probably hit the plane's tail. Along with former Japanese Air Force general Takedo, he believes the plane must have hit the water some three minutes after being hit. (See Rohmer, *Massacre 747,* pp. 114–20.)

33. See *New York Times,* September 4, 9, 10, 12, 18, 21, 23, 27, 28, 29; *Washington Post,* September 17; and *ICAO Report,* pp. 33 ff. The official report concludes: "There was extensive search for the acoustic signal for over two months by vessels from Japan, the United States and the Union of Soviet Socialist Republics. Signals were intermittently received by some search vessels of the United States. However, the recorder was not located in the irregular and very difficult underwater terrain of the Sea of Japan." (*ICAO Report,* p. 28.) The wreckage was officially located at 46°35'N and 141°20'E. Who would have had great interest in either recovering or concealing the digital flight data recorder and the cockpit voice recorder depends, of course, on one's conclusions regarding the innocence or culpability of the jet's crew.

While the details of search and rescue operations need not concern us here, it is worth noting that in the view of all U.S. and Japanese personnel involved, Soviet vessels and Soviet authorities were systematically obstructing efforts of the other powers to locate and retrieve the data and voice recorders, at times resorting to rather unorthodox techniques. For one account of the operations, see Rohmer, *Massacre 747,* pp. 140–47.

On the first anniversary of the incident, Soviet news media asserted that "according to some authoritative reports, the United States has been successful in salvaging the black box [from the debris of KAL 007]." The Soviet news agency Novosti charged that the U.S. was hiding this fact "because what was recorded ... is so incriminating that no amount of editing can change the content." (Cited in *San Francisco Chronicle,* September 1, 1984.) The Soviet media have generally been careful not to make such a claim as an official Soviet allegation but to attribute it to others (e.g., to the American editor of *Microwave Systems News*); ostensibly the U.S. had planned to announce the discovery of the "black box" until it acquainted itself with its contents (something that hardly squares with the premeditated conspiracy version, either). (*Za rubezhom,* no. 27, 1984, p. 11.) Though the question whether either side may have surreptitiously salvaged the plane's recorder has been raised more than once, from all the available information the charge appears to be entirely groundless.

Chapter 2

1. One speculative allegation that "this cannot be discounted" is to be found in an unattributed box accompanying the article by Viktor Belenko, "What *Really* Happened to KAL Flight 007?" *Reader's Digest,* January 1984, p. 77: "According to the Defense Department," it claims, "in each of the past few years the Soviets have made dozens of electronic attempts to dupe and confuse American pilots into flying into forbidden territory where they could be shot at. The practice involves 'meaconing'—the sending of misleading navigational signals from powerful portable transmitters—as well as radar and radio jamming. It continues today, and, in fact, reports of meaconing and jamming increased roughly 20 percent in 1983." The *Reader's Digest* adds that "sophisticated American countermeasures, coupled with special training of air crews, have reduced the effectiveness of this predatory deception. Nevertheless, the Soviets keep trying, hoping to create international incidents which their propagandists can exploit." It is also true that U.S. Federal Aviation Administration maps of this area contain a warning that reads: "Unlisted radio emissions from this area may constitute a navigation hazard or result in border overflight unless unusual precaution is exercised." Whatever the technical capabilities or experiments on the Soviet side, which may well exist, the above passage nonetheless represents a combination of nonsense, hearsay, and propaganda that leads me to dismiss it as a serious interpretation of the incident.

2. *Toronto Globe and Mail,* September 6.

3. See *ICAO Report,* pp. 15–16, 36–37, A7, B1–3.

4. Equally ludicrous was the report that former President Richard M. Nixon had been scheduled to fly to Seoul on this plane and had canceled at the last moment (or, according to one version, had been tipped off by U.S. intelligence not to take the flight—a theory compatible with the notion of the plane's use by "certain circles" in the U.S. to be sacrificed for "catalytic" political purposes). Nixon, along with a number of other American politicians, especially of conservative persuasion, had been invited to the same conference on the 30th anniversary of the U.S.–South Korean defense treaty as Larry McDonald was about to attend—a fact which was reported after the incident. The West German magazine *Quick* "reported" (in its issue of September 8) the sensationalized version of the Nixon story, which TASS promptly picked up, adding that evidently the CIA "did not dare send a former president to his death" and must have alerted him at the last minute. (*Washington Post,* September 25.) Moscow also responded angrily to a column by Jack Anderson which claimed to know that the South Korean airliner forced down by Soviet interceptors over Kola Peninsula in 1978 had been "disoriented" by a Soviet agent on board. (Vladimir Serov, Moscow Radio [TASS] in Russian, September 22, 0922 GMT.)

5. *ICAO Report,* p. 11.

6. Ibid., p. 14. "'Everyone flying Red 20 should use their radar for back-up,' says 747 Captain Chuck Hall of San Diego, who has flown that route for 15 years. Presumably if the KAL pilots had used their weather radar, and if the equipment was working, they would have picked up Soviet landmasses." (*TIME,* September 19, p. 25.)

7. Cf. Douglas B. Feaver, "Flaws Cited in Technology on Korean Jet," *Washington Post,* September 11; *TIME,* September 19, p. 25.

8. *ICAO Report,* p. 45.

9. Ibid., pp. 44–48; Michael Westlake, "On Course for Disaster," *Far Eastern Economic Review,* October 13, p. 29; Kenneth J. Stein, "Human Factors Analyzed in 007 Navigation Error," *Aviation Week and Space Technology,* October 3, p. 165. The Soviet pilots several times described KAL 007's heading as 240 degrees.

10. *ICAO Report,* pp. 49–52; Richard Witkin, "Computer Input Error Suspected in Korean Airliner's Bad Course," *New York Times,* November 17. The same notion was suggested by Admiral Bobby Inman, a respected former deputy director of Central Intelligence. (Robert Manning, "Who Gave the Order?" *Far Eastern Economic Review,* September 15, p. 14.) See also "Soviets' Murderous Military Bungling," *Far Eastern Economic Review,* January 19, 1984, p. 62.

11. ICAO, *Final Report of Investigation* (Doc. C-WP/7809), February 16, 1984; *Report of the Air Navigation Commission* (hereafter cited as ANC *Report*), p. 14.

12. *ICAO Report,* p. 4.

13. Ibid., pp. 7–10. See also ibid., pp. 3–4, 44, 49–52; *New York Times,* September 6, 13, 17, November 17, 1983, and March 21, 1984.

14. *ICAO Report,* pp. 44, G6–9. No doubt, the companies involved much preferred a finding implying human error to one suggesting equipment malfunction.

15. See ibid., Appendix C, for a transcription of communications from KAL 007 to ground stations during the flight as it claimed to be passing over Bethel, NABIE, NEEVA, and NIPPI.

16. All standard maps of the North Pacific used by commercial aircraft carry the clear notation: "WARNING—Aircraft infringing upon non-free flying territory may be fired on without warning."

17. "Stray Jets: The Human Factor," *Science News,* vol. 124, no. 13 (September 24), p. 196; and Richard Rohmer, *Massacre 747* (Markham, Ont., Canada: PaperJacks, 1984), p. 57.

18. *ICAO Report,* Appendix C, p. C9.

19. Ibid., p. 3.

20. Ibid., p. 1.

21. Rohmer, *Massacre 747,* p. 63.

22. Ibid., pp. 30, A15.

23. Murray Sayle, "Charge and Countercharge," *Far Eastern Economic Review,* September 22, p. 28.

24. See Rohmer, *Massacre 747,* pp. 63–70, 202–13; and *Far Eastern Economic Review,* January 19, 1984, p. 63.

25. Rohmer fantasizes: "As a matter of company policy there could be incentive bonuses to those captains and crews that cut corners, jumped lines and saved the company money. A bonus of fifty percent of the saving would not be unreasonable, but perhaps one-third of the saving might be what a prudent, cost-cutting company would offer." (*Massacre 747,* p. 209.)

26. *The Economist,* September 10, p. 34.

27. *ICAO Report,* p. 35.

28. Ibid., pp. 44–45; Sayle, "Charge and Countercharge"; and *TIME,* September 19, p. 25, which stresses that South Korean pilots were particularly sensitive to airspace violations, given the 1978 Soviet downing of a South Korean passenger aircraft (discussed at a later point) and the problems created by the proximity of the demilitarized zone and North Korean airspace near Seoul.

As indicated elsewhere, the B747 had three VHF (very high frequency) transceivers and two HF (high frequency) transceivers, as well as two SSR (secondary surveillance radar) transponders. KAL procedures required one of the VHF radios to be set at 121.5 MHz, the international emergency frequency, and a second radio to be reserved for air traffic control communications. While one of the three VHF radios had been reported out of order on the New York–Anchorage lap, it was tested and found to be functioning at the stopover. VHF communications between KAL 007 and Anchorage ATC seemed to be normal until the plane was beyond the VHF range—something like 150 miles. The record of VHF and HF communications with ground stations (and transmissions relayed by other planes) is available but does not appear to contain any information helpful in our analysis. It is apparently not unusual for aircraft at considerable distance from ground control stations to relay messages by way of other planes. (*ICAO Report,* pp. 11, 17–21, 31, G13–14.) It may be assumed that the pilot was flying the aircraft and the co-pilot handled radio communications (and, indeed, Tokyo radio later identified the voice as that of the co-pilot). The plane was in touch with AMS radio at Kenai, Bethel, St.Paul, and Shemya RCAG by VHF, and with Anchorage and Tokyo by HF. Whatever the plane's difficulties at various times of reaching ground stations (or vice versa), there was never a time during the flight (until it was shot down) when it could not establish radio communications.

29. After flying in a virtually straight line, KAL 007 apparently executed a turn (according to Ogarkov, at 1802 hours), as is also confirmed by some of the remarks of Soviet fighters on the intercepted tapes (though the maneuver may not have covered as much ground as Marshal Ogarkov's well-publicized map suggested). While this indicates that the cockpit crew of KAL 007 was not relying totally on automatic pilot and must have been aware of where they were—or thought they were—there is no single explanation for the particular maneuver which the plane executed. In essence, before reaching Sakhalin it made a

semicircle—not in the direction of Japan, which would have allowed it to stay out of trouble, but in the opposite direction, as if either bypassing Soviet SAM or radar installations at Yuzhno-Sakhalinsk or else intentionally seeking to overfly an area that was otherwise not in its path. Thereafter it turned south again, as if expecting to resume its earlier course, and that is of course when it was finally apprehended by the Soviet interceptors. There is no compelling information that would make it possible to choose among the conflicting hypotheses seeking to explain the maneuver in question.

30. *ICAO Report,* pp. 2, 36.

31. The U.S. government routinely denied any involvement by the Central Intelligence Agency—in the light of earlier history, not a surefire indication that it had in fact not been involved. A quibbler might also maintain that such a denial did not necessarily cover other U.S. government agencies, such as the National Security Agency (NSA).

General George Keegan, former chief of U.S. Air Force intelligence and a prominent "hard-liner," was quoted as commenting after the incident: "I have never failed to be surprised at how careless the Koreans are, despite the risks of flying near Soviet airspace." He said the Koreans had flown "too close" to Soviet territory for too long, hence "what happened . . . they invited." This surprisingly eager condemnation of the Koreans is likely to have provoked some puzzled wonderment whether they were to serve as a lightning rod to deflect suspicion from U.S. intelligence.

32. Thus, A. Leont'ev wrote in *Krasnaia Zvezda* (September 6): "In the light of recent events it is becoming particularly obvious that Washington needed the criminal provocation in the Far East to raise even higher the pitch of military hysteria, the arms race, and preparations for war." Ogarkov in his televised press conference remarked: "A civilian plane was chosen for it deliberately, disregarding or possibly counting on loss of human life." In the words of a Soviet veteran Washington correspondent, Melor Sturua: "If the incident had not happened, it would have been necessary to invent it. . . . The act of provocation concocted in the Washington corridors of power was, so to speak, a 'cluster' provocation. It was one more missile to torpedo the relaxation of international tension." (*Izvestiia,* September 7.)

33. R. W. Johnson, "007: License to Kill?" *The Guardian,* December 17.

34. Soviet statements have insisted that over Kamchatka both ground and air interrogation of KAL 007 yielded no result and that over Sakhalin at least one of the interceptors sought to contact the aircraft on IFF frequency, and again in vain. The latter occurrence is confirmed by the tape released by the United States. As normally only military aircraft have the IFF equipment, this suggests what the Soviet pilot assumed the intruder to be. However, the failure of KAL 007 to respond to the IFF signal is not significant.

While the plane's crew might have turned off the transponder to disguise its location, American and Japanese military sources have claimed that the jet's transponder was functioning both when it left Anchorage and when it came within radar range of Wakkanai. It emits a coded electronic signal that permits identifying the plane on a radar screen, and some American intelligence analysts had assumed—erroneously, it would appear—that Soviet monitors could decode it, too.

35. There is by now an extensive literature of memoirs and hearings (such as the Church Committee of the U.S. Senate) on CIA and NSA activities, in addition to secondary works such as Harry A. Rositzke, *The CIA's Secret Operations* (New York: Reader's Digest, 1977); James Bamford, *The Puzzle Palace* (Boston: Houghton Mifflin, 1983); and Robert Borosage et al., eds., *The CIA File* (New York: Grossman, 1976). Rudolf Braunburg, a Lufthansa pilot, writing in *Deutsches Allgemeines Sonntagsblatt,* September 7, is cited by R. W. Johnson ("007: License to Kill?") as describing the purposive mixing of military and civilian planes and missions. See also A. Peshcherin, "Shpion za oblakami," *Sovetskaia Rossiia,* December 11.

Soviet media had a field day using all possible and some impossible allegations and insinuations about ostensible CIA connections with Korean Air Lines. The most extreme (and specific) of such articles, by a Colonel K. Borisov, "A Branch of American Intelligence: South Korean Airlines in the Service of the CIA," alleged that "in the early seventies a top-secret agreement was concluded between the CIA . . . and KAL on the use of its passenger aircraft for carrying out reconnaissance of Soviet territory." Colonel Chun, the 007's pilot, allegedly "boasted to some close friends that he was carrying out special assignments for U.S. intelligence and he even showed some of them his aircraft's spy equipment." (*Krasnaia Zvezda,* September 16; trans. in *CDSP,* Vol. XXXV, no. 37, pp. 9–10; *FBIS,* September 19, pp. DD13–16.) In fact, of course, Chun did not have "his" plane—different personnel were assigned to different aircraft, which, moreover, were piloted by different men on the New York-Anchorage and Anchorage-Seoul runs.

See Christopher Robbins, *Air America* (New York: Putnam, 1979), for an account of the CIA-sponsored airline system. For a popular summary of the intelligence-gathering system, including the reconnaissance satellites, see Michael Krepon and Barry Blechman, "America's Global Lie Detector," *Popular Mechanics,* February 1984, pp. 86–89.

36. *ICAO Report,* p. G13 and p. 39, which suggests, correctly: "Although KE007 was likely to have been beyond the coverage limits [about 200 nautical miles] of the [Shemya Air Force Base] radar, the mere absence of its radar response would have been grounds for corrective actions had the SSR radar been employed for such purposes."

37. *ICAO Report,* pp. C5, C7, and F3. The Chief of Staff of the Air Defense Forces, Colonel General Semion Romanov, described the altitude of the "violating aircraft" as "between eight and ten thousand meters." Marshal Ogarkov, in his press conference, also reported it sighted initially at 8,000 meters.

38. *ICAO Report,* pp. 38–40.

39. *Aviation Week and Space Technology,* September 12, p. 20.

40. There is one curious and unexplained statement in the Air Navigation Commission's report to the ICAO. It reports that the jetliner's "SSR transponder was operating on departure from Anchorage and when the aircraft appeared on the Wakkanai radar." (*ANC Report,* p. 13.) It is not clear whether this is meant to imply that the radar crew at Wakkanai was able to decode the aircraft's identification.

41. *ICAO Report,* p. 38.

42. Philip Taubman, in *New York Times,* September 5.

43. Ibid., September 14. For the fullest case, see David Pearson, "K.A.L.007: What the U.S. Knew And When We Knew It," *The Nation,* August 18–25, 1984, which states (p. 112) that "the RC-135 carries an electronic surveillance system that automatically acquires and identifies signals from both ground-based and airborne radar" and thus would have been virtually certain to have identified KAL 007 prior to its penetration of Soviet airspace (if it had not been otherwise informed of its flight).

The Pearson piece received a good deal of publicity and was the subject of a full-page advertisement by *The Nation,* billed as a "Memorandum to the press and the public" (*New York Times,* October 25, 1984), affirming that "The Nation Magazine believes that the official U.S. version is not credible." Assistant Secretary of State Richard Burt dismissed it as "pure baloney." Others in Washington sought to provide a more substantive rebuttal. (*New York Times,* October 28, 1984.)

44. Tom Bernard and T. Edward Eskelson, "U.S. Spy Plane Capable of Interceding in Attack on Korean Jet," *Denver Post,* September 13.

45. The *ANC Report* states (p. 13):

The Commission was informed that

(a) the handling staff in New York and Anchorage had free access to all parts of the aircraft and none of these personnel reported any unusual equipment or structural changes;

(b) the flight schedules of the airframe showed it did not adhere to any set pattern;

(c) the point of view of the manufacturer was that any modification to equip the airframe for intelligence gathering purposes would require substantial outage from service, and service records proved that this had not been the case.

46. According to Leslie Gelb, "the only imaging system that works at higher altitudes at night is something called synthetic aperture radar. This emits no waves or signals. Instead, it absorbs energy radiated from the earth and buildings and other ground structures. This is said to be used on SR-71's and U-2 spy planes. The equipment involved is fairly large and is said to take up a lot of space. If the Central Intelligence Agency had equipped the Korean airliner in this way, the cost would have been several million dollars, and Congress would have had to approve the expenditure. It is always possible that the agency disguised the

money, but Congressional auditing of the CIA budget is rigorous." (*New York Times,* September 26.) See also Andrew Cockburn, *The Threat: Inside the Soviet Military Machine* (New York: Vintage, 1984), p. 370.

47. P. Kirsanov, "Fakty izoblichaiut Vashington," *Pravda,* September 20; English trans. in *CDSP,* Vol. XXXV, no. 38, pp. 6–7. See also "Flight 007: Many Questions Remain a Year After the Incident," *New York Times,* September 1, 1984; and the section entitled "Activities of the intelligence services of the United States," in the Soviet "preliminary report" to the ICAO investigation team, in *ICAO Report,* Appendix F, p. F11. As indicated earlier, some aspects of the Kirsanov "circumstantial" scenario do not check out at all, e.g., the 40-minute delay in Anchorage. This also includes the Soviet charge that KAL 007 had picked up additional (and suspect) "personnel" at Anchorage and was heading for Seoul with a total flight crew of twenty-nine—well in excess of normal crew size—according to Soviet charges, to operate intelligence equipment. Apparently, it was standard practice for KAL (as for other airlines) to give free flights home, on a space-available basis, to flight personnel who were off duty at points serviced by the airline, as was the case here. Like other Soviet commentators, Kirsanov also claimed that Colonel Chun was known "for his links to American intelligence," as was the co-pilot.

A White House spokesman promptly dismissed Kirsanov's charges as "untrue" and "without foundation." (*New York Times,* September 20.)

Bernard and Eskelson ("U.S. Spy Plane") write: "It has been our experience that, on occasion, NSA adjusts the orbits of RC-135s so that they will intentionally penetrate the airspace of a target nation. This is ordered for the purpose of bringing a target country's air defense systems into a state of alert. This allows NSA to analyze these fully activated systems for potential flaws and weaknesses."

48. See Pearson, "K.A.L.007."

49. See, in particular, the widely reported article by P. Q. Mann [pseud.], "Reassessing the Sakhalin Incident," *Defence Attaché* (London), no. 3 (June 1984), pp. 41–56; reprinted in Russian (with some changes and deletions) in *Za rubezhom* (Moscow), no. 27, 1984. It is true that a photograph taken from another flight of the space shuttle, some months later, was "leaked" from NASA files and made its way into print, showing the area of Petropavlovsk-on-Kamchatka, including some of the military and naval installations there. See "Mission 9 Astronauts Photographed Soviet Submarine, Fighter Bases at Petropavlovsk," *Aviation Week and Space Technology,* March 19, 1984, p. 17. However, the "P. Q. Mann" argument concerned electronic intelligence, not photography, in any event.

The *Defence Attaché* article also makes several extravagant assertions, including the possibility of a secret Soviet-American deal by which, after the KAL 007 incident, the U.S. agreed to demilitarize the space shuttle in return for Moscow not revealing all it knew about the flight. This appears quite nonsensical.

The guidance sent to overseas posts by the United States Information Agency suggested, in what must have been one of its more ludicrous efforts, that the (rather technical and nonpolitical, and in fact by no means pro-Soviet) *Defence Attaché* article must have been Soviet-inspired, probably to take attention off the case of dissident physicist Andrei Sakharov.

In a rather surprising development, Korean Air Lines sued *Defence Attaché* for implying that KAL 007 had been on a spy mission, and in November 1984 accepted a public apology and a "substantial" sum of money from the magazine to settle the case. (*New York Times,* November 20, 1984.) Naturally, the legal settlement hardly affects the scholarly analysis of the case. At the same time, the South Korean authorities withdrew permission for the production of a film dealing with the jetliner episode; the producer reported having been told that South Korean cooperation could jeopardize Soviet participation in the 1988 Summer Olympics in Seoul. (*Los Angeles Times,* November 16, 1984.)

50. *Washington Post,* September 16; *San Francisco Examiner,* September 25.

51. Cf. William Safire, "Sticks and Stones," *Washington Post,* September 8.

52. See *Aviation Week and Space Technology,* April 23, 1984. The most thorough discussion of the subject, though questionable in a number of particular assertions, is Pearson, "K.A.L.007," pp. 105–24.

53. Pearson, "K.A.L.007"; Bamford, *Puzzle Palace;* Anthony Sampson, "What Happened to Flight 007?" *Parade Magazine,* April 22, 1984, pp. 12–13.

54. "P.Q. Mann" makes the case, after detailing several (much) earlier instances in which U.S. military reconnaissance missions were shot down, that "if the U.S. intelligence services planned the Korean incident, they would have been in no doubt that they could not achieve their aims with a military aircraft." But presumably they would have wanted to test the effect of a military aircraft on Soviet air defenses; hence the intentional coincidence with the RC-135 flight shortly before KAL 007 reached Soviet airspace. (Mann, "Sakhalin Incident," p. 48.) This coincides with the Pearson argument, cited earlier.

Chapter 3

1. For an interesting and sophisticated discussion of alternative approaches and methodologies, see Stephen M. Meyer, "Soviet National Security Decisionmaking: What Do We Know and What Do We Understand?" in Jiri Valenta and William C. Potter, eds., *Soviet Decisionmaking for National Security* (London: George Allen & Unwin, 1984), chap. 11.

I take it to be a fact that the South Korean jet was shot down by a Soviet fighter plane—a fact established both by the available tapes and, ultimately, by Soviet admission. I am therefore prepared to dismiss as without merit the suggestion that the aircraft was destroyed by a bomb planted on board KAL 007 and set off by remote control on orders from U.S. authorities to prevent the evidence of an intelligence mission from falling into Soviet hands. (This version, broadcast by Radio Moscow on August 25, 1984, was attributed to an interview in the Italian Newspaper *Il Messaggero* with John Keppel, a former U.S. foreign service officer, who did indeed seek to investigate the incident but claimed to have mentioned this possibility merely as the least probable explanation. See *San Francisco Examiner,* August 26, 1984.)

2. *ICAO Report,* Appendix F, p. F3. See also the Marshal Ogarkov press conference, *Pravda,* September 10.

3. Michael Westlake, "On Course for Disaster," *Far Eastern Economic Review,* October 13, p. 32.

4. Interview with Colonel General Nikolai Moskvitelev, commander of PVO aviation, Moscow domestic television, 2320 GMT, September 10 (*FBIS:USSR,* September 12, p. DD36).

5. Letter of CPSU to Japanese Communist Party, September 12, in *Akahata* (Tokyo), September 22.

6. Boris Reznik, in *Izvestiia,* September 12 (*FBIS:USSR,* September 12, pp. DD37–38).

7. David Shribman, "U.S. Experts Say Soviet Didn't See Jet Was Civilian," *New York Times,* October 7.

8. V. Zakharov, in *Pravda,* September 7. According to an unauthenticated report, an unidentified Soviet official stated later that "two of three radar installations on the Kamchatka Peninsula were not working." Actually there are a good many more than two or three radar installations there. He is also reported to have said that the air defense command on Kamchatka had responded in confusion. (Anthony Robinson, in *Financial Times,* October 13.)

9. On Soviet practice, see Ralph Ostrich, "Aeroflot," *Armed Forces Journal International,* May 1981, pp. 38–56.

10. Ogarkov press conference, *Pravda,* September 10.

11. One of the Soviet spokespersons, Viktor Linnik, apparently got himself into an awkward situation by being quoted in England as doubting whether KAL 007 was on a spying mission and describing the Soviet air defense crews as "trigger-happy." He protested to have the record revised and righted. (London Press Association, September 22, *FBIS:USSR,* September 22, pp. DD1–2; *Washington Post,* September 22; *New York Times,* September 24.) For the remarks by Viktor Afanas'yev, editor of *Pravda,* in the same vein, see below.

12. Clarence A. Robinson, Jr., "U.S. Says Soviets Knew Korean Air Lines 747 Was Commercial Flight," *Aviation Week and Space Technology,* September 12; also *TIME,* September 19, p. 26.

13. Shribman, "U.S. Experts."

14. Robinson, "U.S. Says."

15. Shribman, "U.S. Experts."

16. Andrew Cockburn, *The Threat* (New York: Vintage, 1984), p. 368.

17. "Soviets' Murderous Military Bungling," *Far Eastern Economic Review,* January 19, 1984, p. 64.

18. There is, strangely, some disagreement about weather conditions over Kamchatka and Sakhalin. The *ICAO Report* seems most reliable here, reporting on the basis of satellite pictures and surface observations that, at the time of the passage over the area by KAL 007, there was extensive cloud coverage over southern Kamchatka and that over southern Sakhalin there were mostly overcast low clouds, with scattered medium and high clouds. Over Sakhalin the aircraft should have been in moonlight, approximately 45 percent of the moon disk illuminated, about 66° above the horizon. (See *ICAO Report,* Appendix B.)

19. It has been alleged that the PVO has "at least one regiment" at the ready, at Dolinsk-Sokol airbase on Sakhalin. See Richard Rohmer, *Massacre 747* (Markham, Ont., Canada: PaperJacks, 1984), pp. 90, 96.

20. It is discussed later in this chapter.

21. *Aviation Week and Space Technology,* September 12, p. 20. Nonsensical stories about Soviet officers executed for the Murmansk incident have been circulated, apparently by defectors. One U.S. intelligence expert claimed to have personal knowledge that "six colonels of air defense forces were shot" in the Far East for failure to shoot down U.S. aircraft, on unspecified occasions—a rather absurd assertion. (*New York Times,* September 2.)

22. Ogarkov press conference, *Pravda,* September 10. The latter reference is not entirely clear. It may refer to the jet's climbing from 33,000 to 35,000 feet, which confused the pursuing Su-15; and to its change of direction to the right as it approached Sakhalin.

23. On the PVO, see Cockburn, *The Threat,* chap. 13; and especially David R. Jones, "Air Defense Forces," in *Soviet Armed Forces Review Annual,* Vol. VI (1982), pp. 132–95, and Richard G. Breighner, "Air Defense Forces," in ibid., Vol. VII (1984), pp. 158–65. "The budget battles give [PVO] an added incentive to encourage the perception that Soviet borders are under constant danger of penetration or attack." (*Newsweek,* September 19, p. 24.)

24. Viktor Belenko, "What *Really* Happened to KAL 007," *Reader's Digest,* January 1984.

25. For the Law of the Border, see below.

26. According to Soviet defectors and emigrés, every unidentified aircraft that comes within sixty miles of Soviet airspace must be reported to the national command center of the PVO. There are some misconceptions in Rohmer's account of Soviet military decision-making. (*Massacre 747,* pp. 95–96, 185–91.) He also refers repeatedly to "Biya" as the location of the "regional" command of the PVO and speaks of the "attribution by Ogarkov to the Biya commander" of the decision to shoot down the plane. (Ibid., pp. 8, 36, 42, 95, 185–89, 206.) In fact, Ogarkov never refers to Biya, whose existence is unknown and which is unidentified on any available map or gazetteer.

27. Dusko Doder, in *Washington Post,* October 5.

28. Victor Belenko, "What *Really* Happened to KAL Flight 007," *Reader's Digest,* January 1984, pp. 72–78. See also Dimitri Simes, in *Washington Post,* September 2; and Moskvitelev interview, Moscow Domestic Television, September 10, (*FBIS: USSR,* September 12, p. DD39).

29. Moscow Domestic Television, 1300 GMT, September 10 (*FBIS: USSR,* September 12, p. DD33).

30. William J. Hughes, "Aerial Intrusion By Civil Airlines and the Use of Force," *Journal of Air Law and Commerce,* vol. 35 (1980), pp. 595–620.

31. "Law of the Union of Soviet Socialist Republics on the USSR State Border," *Pravda,* November 26, 1982, English trans. in *CDSP,* Vol. XXXIV, no. 51, pp. 15–20.

For a general discussion of the legal aspects of the case, see Philippe Sands, "The Legal Fallout from KAL 007," *International Review* (Harvard), November 1983, pp. 44–45; Gérard Fouilloux, "The Destruction of the K.A.L. 747 and the Law," *ITA Magazine,* November 1983, pp. 56–69, and December 1983, pp. 36–51; "Documents Concerning the Korean Air Lines Incidents," *International Legal Materials,* September 1983, pp. 1109–

1220; and also Karin Schmid, "Zum neuen Grenzgesetz der USSR," *Berichte* des Bundesinstituts für ostwissenschaftliche und internationale Studien (Köln), no. 18 (1984). For well-orchestrated arguments by Soviet jurists that Soviet behavior in the KAL 007 crisis was in conformity with Soviet and international law, see "Zashchita granits—suverennoe pravo gosudarstv," *Pravda,* September 8; Moscow radio in Russian, 1800 GMT, September 6; 0900 GMT, September 7; and 0731 GMT, September 8 (*FBIS:USSR,* September 7, pp. C14–15, and September 8, pp. C5 –6); G. Tunkin, in *Izvestiia,* September 9. For the ICAO resolution, see *ICAO Bulletin,* November 1983, p. 11.

32. "Preliminary Information on the Progress of the USSR Investigation into the Accident to a South Korean Aeroplane on 1 September 1983," Appendix F to ICAO Document C-WP/7764, pp. 7–10.

33. *ICAO Report,* pp. 2, 3, 40.

34. See ibid., p. 2.

35. See Sands, "Legal Fallout."

36. "Interception Procedures Used by USSR," instructions issued May 27, 1980, Appendix H, *ICAO Report.*

37. For sophisticated discussions of the general problem, see Robert Jervis, *Perception and Misperception in International Politics* (Princeton, N.J.: Princeton University Press, 1976); and Ole Holsti, "Cognitive Process Approaches to Decision-Making," *American Behavioral Scientist,* Vol. XX, no. 1 (1976), pp. 11–32.

38. On Soviet political culture, see, e.g., Archie Brown and Jack Gray, eds., *Political Culture and Political Change in Communist States* (London: Macmillan, 1977); Robert C. Tucker, "Culture, Political Culture, and Communist Society," *Political Science Quarterly,* June 1973; and Stephen White, *Political Culture and Soviet Politics* (London: Macmillan, 1979), although some of their propositions are highly debatable. For purposes of the present inquiry, see Vladimir Petrov, "Danger, Soviet Border—Don't Touch," *Washington Post,* September 11. And see Alexander George, "The Operational Code: A Neglected Approach," in *International Studies Quarterly,* Vol. XIII (1969), pp. 190–222.

39. Indeed, according to Jack Anderson a secret report by Secretary of Defense Caspar Weinberger to President Reagan, entitled "U.S. Interests and Objectives in the Asia-Pacific Area," approved by the Joint Chiefs of Staff, stresses the immense Soviet potential and (according to the same source) asserts that the Soviet Union has gained nuclear supremacy in the Pacific. (Jack Anderson, "Soviet Strength in the Pacific," *Washington Post,* September 11.) See also Yossef Bodansky, "What the Soviets Are So Anxious to Conceal," *Business Week,* September 19; Michael Klare, "Asia: Theatre of Nuclear War," *South* (London), no. 37 (November 1983), pp. 9–14; and Rohmer, *Massacre 747,* pp. 26, 91.

40. See Klare, "Asia"; William·V. Kennedy and S. Michael deGyurky, "An Alternative Strategy for the 80's," *National Defense,* July/August 1983, pp. 47–54; Aleksandr Bovin, in *Izvestiia,* September 13, trans. as "Siberia, the Boeing, and a Little About Hospitality," *FBIS:USSR,* September 13, p. DD1.

41. *Soviet Armed Forces Review Annual,* Vol. VII (1984), p. 321.

42. By one calculation, all in all more than twenty-five aircraft engaged in electronic surveillance were attacked or destroyed—mostly in the 1950s and '60s. This included a few incidents over Germany, at least two over Soviet Armenia, and several involving North Korea, with most of the others in or off the Soviet Far East and the Sea of Japan. The KAL 007 incident provided an occasion for Soviet journalists to trot out earlier cases to establish the pattern of American responsibility. The following may serve as a typical sample:

> The lives of 269 people have been added to the list of victims of U.S. imperialism and its tool—the CIA. . . . Beyond any doubt the methods used in organizing the present provocation are not new. This kind of thing has happened before. Exactly 25 years ago, in September 1958 . . . a U.S. C-130 aircraft violated the Soviet border and intruded into the airspace of Soviet Armenia. Following the publication in the Soviet Union of the announcement that a U.S. Hercules C-130 caught fire and burned up above the territory of the Armenian SSR, Washington tried to use its own method for misleading world public opinion: the U.S. authorities launched a smear campaign against the USSR. An account was even concocted according to which the Soviet fighter allegedly "enticed" the U.S. military plane across the border on to its own territory and then shot it

down.... Less than three years later, in the spring of 1960, a U-2 spy plane was shot down over Sverdlovsk.... There are many similarities between that provocation and the present one. Above all, the fact that Soviet air defense was totally ignorant of what was on board the intruding aircraft, which penetrated 500 km into Soviet airspace by night: electronic espionage equipment, or nuclear bombs, or cruise missiles—it was capable of carrying at least two dozen of them. (Igor Sinitsin, in *Sovetskaia Rossiia,* September 9; trans. in *FBIS:USSR,* September 13, pp. DD13–14.)

43. For a listing, see U.S. Senate, *Congressional Record,* pp. S 12128–30 (September 14, 1983).

44. V. James Bamford, *The Puzzle Palace* (Boston: Houghton Mifflin, 1982), p. 138.

45. *New York Times,* September 15, 1958, February 6 and 8, 1959; Bamford, *Puzzle Palace,* pp. 138–43, 178–84, which also has the best general discussion of the use of signal intelligence by the U.S. National Security Agency.

46. Israeli journalist Theodore Levite has been quoted as relating that the incident was the indirect result of Soviet MiG-15s trying to intercept a U.S. Air Force Constellation flying reconnaissance missions near the Yugoslav-Bulgarian border. The El Al plane shot down was apparently erroneously taken to be the U.S. plane in question. (*Far Eastern Economic Review,* January 19, 1984, p. 64.) See also Robert Jervis, *Perception and Misperception in International Politics* (Princeton, N.J.: Princeton University Press, 1976), pp. 215–16.

For Soviet allegations of British and NATO responsibility for other crashes, trotted out after the KAL disaster, see Moscow radio in English, 2010 GMT, September 21 (*FBIS:USSR,* September 22, p. DD5).

47. Moscow radio in English, 0842 GMT, September 23 (*FBIS:USSR,* September 26, pp. DD5–6). See also *TIME,* September 12, p. 17.

48. Robert Scheer, "Outrage Over the Korean Jet Can Mislead Us," *Los Angeles Times,* September 18.

49. *The Guardian* (London), April 26, 1978; *New York Times,* April 21–24, 1978; *Aviation Week and Space Technology,* May 1, 1978; *Pravda,* April 22 and 30, 1978; *New York Times,* September 9 (interview with Captain Kim Chang Kyu); Anthony Paul, "Shot Down Over Russia! The Mysterious Saga of Flight 902," *Reader's Digest,* November 1978, pp. 138–44; Cockburn, *The Threat,* pp. 362–63.

50. Some of the more insightful journalistic reporting on the KAL 007 crisis made reference to some or all of these traits. See, e.g., Serge Schmemann, "Russian Reaction: Old Fears Revived," *New York Times,* September 6; Michael Dobbs, "Plane Incident Illustrates Historic Soviet Insecurity," *Washington Post,* September 19; Ned Temko, "How Soviets Think: The Unknown Factor in the Superpower Equation," *Christian Science Monitor,* November 18.

51. *New York Times,* October 28.

52. BBC Domestic Service, 1200 GMT, September 18 (*FBIS:USSR,* September 19, pp. DD17–20). The Russian for *guilty* might be more properly rendered here as *responsible.*

53. Several stories even in leading papers were clearly inspired by calculated "leaks" from within the Administration, and the Pentagon in particular. See, e.g., Walter J. Mossberg, "Soviet Military, Civilian Leaders Clash Over Downed KAL Plane," *Wall Street Journal,* September 27, which argued that "U.S. analysts suspect that the airliner incident ... may have placed major strains on the coalition that brought Soviet President Yuri Andropov to power last fall." See also Robert J. Toth, in the *Los Angeles Times,* October 3, who reported on a meeting specially convened by Secretary Shultz on this question. Henry Kissinger was also quoted as having referred to the possible "beginning of a kind of Soviet Bonapartism"—a most unlikely development, and one whose probability was surely not enhanced by the KAL 007 crisis, from which the military emerged with little added glory. For a more balanced analysis, see Cynthia A. Roberts, "Is the Soviet Military Rising in Power?" *New York Times,* February 9, 1984.

54. Westlake, "On Course for Disaster," p. 32.

55. *New York Times,* September 18.

56. Walter Pincus, "The Soviets Had the Wrong Stuff," *Washington Post,* September 18.

57. *Washington Post,* October 5; and *New York Times,* October 8. It is true that the "incompetence" theme can be overdone. For two reactions to it, see Benjamin Lambeth, "Is Soviet Air Defense Fearsomely Inept?" *Los Angeles Times,* October 21; and Yitzhak Tara-

sulo, "Is Soviet Radar Really That Bad?" *Armed Forces Journal International,* February 1984, pp. 70–74.

58. As an astute British commentator wrote vividly, the senior Soviet military commander must have said to himself: "The standing regulations say, 'Shoot.' If I obey the rules of engagement, nobody can blame me. I shall have done my duty. If I do not, I may be for the chop. So 'Shoot.'" (David Watt, "No Evil Intent, Just Obeying the Book," *The Times* [London], September 9.)

Chapter 4

1. I am grateful to Robert Legvold for suggesting such a comparison of priorities.

2. For two useful discussions of the Soviet handling, see Peter Kenez, "How Moscow Handled the 007 Affair," *The New Leader,* October 31, pp. 10–12; and Lawrence Sherwin, "The KAL Incident: Analysis of a Soviet Propaganda Campaign," Radio Liberty Research Publications, No. RL 371/83, October 4. See also Serge Schmemann, in the *New York Times,* September 14; and the interesting discussion of the Soviet media treatment of the events, in Peter Kenez, "The Lessons of 007," in Joseph Gordon, ed., *Psychological Operations, East and West* (Boulder, Colo.: Westview Press, 1985, forthcoming).

3. *New York Times,* September 4; Alain Jacob, "Circonstances atténuantes," *Le Monde,* September 10.

4. Michael Dobbs, "Plane Incident Illustrates Historic Soviet Insecurity," *Washington Post,* September 19.

5. Dimitri K. Simes, "Beyond the Cost of the 269 Lives," *New York Times,* September 11.

6. Joseph Kraft, "Ending the KAL Affair," *Washington Post,* September 13.

7. Simes, "Beyond the Cost." For examples of the right-wing critique, see George F. Will, "Needed: A Policy of Punishment," *Newsweek,* September 26; Richard Pipes, "After Death in the Skies, What Now?" *Los Angeles Times,* September 6; Robert Conquest, "Brutality and Deceit: So What's New?" *Washington Post,* September 11; and Patrick J. Buchanan, "U.S. a 'Pitiful, Helpless Giant'?" *Human Events,* October 1, p. 835.

8. See also James Reston, "The Politics of Fear," *New York Times,* September 7.

9. Alexander George, ed., *Managing U.S.-Soviet Rivalry: Problems of Crisis Prevention* (Boulder, Colo.: Westview Press, 1983), p. 2.

10. *New York Times,* October 8.

11. It is unclear whether the transfer of Colonel General Semion Romanov from the position of chief of staff (and first deputy commander) of the PVO to the position of Soviet representative of the Joint Supreme Command of the Warsaw Pact forces to the army of the German Democratic Republic constituted such a demotion. As was seen above, Romanov had played a role in the handling of the KAL 007 incident. He had taken over the new position in East Germany at the beginning of May 1984, and on May 22 *Krasnaia Zvezda* reported that he had died "in the line of duty." (*Neues Deutschland,* May 5–6, 1984; *Krasnaia Zvezda,* May 22, 1984; *New York Times,* May 23, 1984.) Rumors circulating in West Germany spoke of his death as a suicide, but there has been no known substantiation for such surmises. On the other hand, other senior officers involved in the jetliner episode were promoted. Thus, General Vladimir Govorov, who had been commander in chief of the Far Eastern theater since 1980, was listed in June 1984 as a deputy minister of defense of the USSR. (Peter Kruzhin, "Govorov Becomes a Deputy Minister of Defense," Radio Liberty Research Publications, RL 272/84, July 16, 1984.)

12. Colonel V. Sych, "Signal prozvuchal noch'iu," *Krasnaia Zvezda,* October 16; Colonel General of Aviation S. Golubev, "Zadacha gosudarstvennoi vazhnosti," *Aviatsiia i Kosmonavtika,* no. 1 (January 1984), pp. 1–3; *New York Times,* January 8, 1984. It is unlikely that the increased punishment prescribed for military offenses is related to this episode. (See Peter Kruzhin, "Severer Punishment for Military Offenses," Radio Liberty Research Publications, RL 86/84, February 21, 1984.)

13. *Newsweek,* January 23, 1984, p. 36.

14. See, e.g., *Trud,* April 7, 1984; *New York Times,* April 8, 1984.

15. ICAO, News Release, PIO 6/84; *New York Times,* March 7, 1984. See the monthly *ICAO Bulletin* for summaries of the agency's activities relating to the KAL 007 episode.

The amendment to the Chicago Convention, adopted at the Extraordinary Session of the ICAO Assembly in April–May 1984, provides, among other things:

(a) The contracting States recognize that every State must refrain from resorting to the use of weapons against civil aircraft in flight and that, in case of interception, the lives of persons on board and the safety of aircraft must not be endangered. . . .

(b) The contracting States recognize that every State, in the exercise of its sovereignty, is entitled to require the landing at some designated airport of a civil aircraft flying above its territory without authority or if there are reasonable grounds to conclude that it is being used for any purpose inconsistent with the aims of this Convention. (ICAO, "Protocol Relating to an Amendment to the Convention . . . , 10 May 1984," Doc. 9436.)

16. *Pravda,* September 28; *New York Times,* September 29.

17. See Strobe Talbott, *The Russians and Reagan* (New York: Vintage, 1984), pp. 78–85.

18. Bernard Gwertzman, "U.S. Aides Worried Over Soviet Ties," *New York Times,* October 23; Michael Dobbs, "Damage to U.S.-Soviet Relations Is Not Expected to Heal Soon," *Washington Post,* September 25. It is regrettable that there were no Congressional hearings or public inquiries concerning the KAL 007 episode.

19. See, e.g., *Pravda,* August 26–September 4, 1984; *Za rubezhom,* nos. 27 and 35 (1984); *New York Times,* August 31, September 1, 1984.

20. *New York Times,* March 21, 1984.

21. "Russians Said to Use New Codes," *Washington Post,* September 9; *TIME,* September 19, p. 14.

22. For technical discussions of the psychological problems involved, see the papers in Daniel Kahneman, Paul Slovic, and Amos Tversky, eds., *Judgment Under Uncertainty: Heuristics and Biases* (Cambridge, England: Cambridge University Press, 1982).

23. See the excellent discussion in Robert Jervis, *Perception and Misperception in International Politics* (Princeton, N.J.: Princeton University Press, 1976), especially chap. 8.

24. Ole R. Holsti, "Theories of Crisis Decision Making," in Paul Gordon Lauren, ed., *Diplomacy: New Approaches in History, Theory, and Policy* (New York: Free Press, 1979), p. 101; and Charles Hermann, *Crises in Foreign Policy* (New York: Bobbs-Merrill, 1969).

25. Thomas C. Schelling, ed., *Arms and Influence* (New Haven: Yale University Press, 1966); Glenn H. Snyder and Paul Diesing, *Conflict Among Nations* (Princeton, N.J.: Princeton University Press, 1977); Paul Gorden Lauren, "Theories of Bargaining with Threats of Force: Deterrence and Coercive Diplomacy," in Lauren, ed., *Diplomacy,* pp. 186 ff.

26. Cf. Alexander George et al., eds., *The Limits of Coercive Diplomacy* (Boston: Little, Brown, 1971).

Bibliography

Serial Publications (since September 1, 1983)

Aviation Week and Space Technology (Washington, D.C.)
Current Digest of the Soviet Press (Columbus, Ohio)
The Economist (London)
Far Eastern Economic Review (Hong Kong)
Foreign Broadcast Intelligence Service (FBIS), *Daily Report: USSR* and *Far East: Japan* (Washington, D.C.)
ICAO Bulletin (Montreal)
Izvestiia (Moscow)
Japan Times Weekly (Tokyo)
Krasnaia Zvezda (Moscow)
Literaturnaia Gazeta (Moscow)
Newsweek (New York)
New York Times (New York)
Pravda (Moscow)
TIME (New York)
Washington Post (Washington, D.C.)
Za rubezhom (Moscow)

Books, Articles, and Papers

Baber, Asa. "Killing Us Softly With Their Song." *Playboy,* March 1984, pp. 50–51.

Bamford, James. "The Last Flight of KAL 007." *Washington Post Magazine,* January 8, 1984.

Bamford, V. James. *The Puzzle Palace.* Boston: Houghton Mifflin, 1983.

Belenko, Viktor. "What *Really* Happened to KAL Flight 007." *Reader's Digest,* January 1984, pp. 72–78.

Bernard, Tom, and T. Edward Eskelson. "U.S. Spy Plane Capable of Interceding in Attack on Korean Jet." *Denver Post,* September 13, 1983.

[Bialer, Seweryn.] "Andropov Has Displayed Great Ineptness." *U.S. News and World Report,* September 26, 1983, p. 36.

Bodansky, Yossef. "What the Soviets Are So Anxious to Conceal." *Business Week,* September 19, 1983.

Cockburn, Andrew. *The Threat: Inside the Soviet Military Machine.* Rev. ed. New York: Vintage, 1984.

"Documents Concerning the Korean Air Lines Incident." American Society of International Law, *International Legal Materials,* 1983, pp. 1109–1220.

Fouilloux, Gérard. "The Destruction of the KAL 747 and the Law." *ITA Magazine,* November 1983, pp. 56–69, and December 1983, pp. 36–51.

Gillette, Robert. "Flight 007—a Soviet Policy of Distortion." *Los Angeles Times,* October 26, 1983.

———. "Soviets' Public Relations Disaster a Propaganda Coup at Home." *Los Angeles Times,* September 8, 1983.

Golubev, S., Colonel General. "Zadacha gosudarstvennoi vazhnosti." *Aviatsiia i kosmonavtika,* no. 1 (January 1984), pp. 1–3.

Holloway, David. "Soviets Showed Aggression, Ineptitude Downing Plane." *San Jose Mercury News,* September 14, 1983.

Hughes, William J. "Aerial Intrusion by Civil Airlines and the Use of Force." *Journal of Air Law and Commerce,* vol. 35 (1980), pp. 595–620.

International Civil Aviation Organization (ICAO), Montreal, Council. Document C-WP/7764: *Final Report of Investigation as Required in the Council Resolution of 16 September 1983* and attachments (December 2, 1983). Includes as Appendix F: "Preliminary Information on the Progress of the USSR Investigation . . ."; and as Appendix G: Republic of Korea, Incident Investigation Committee, "Interim Report on Incident Investigation."

————, Montreal, Air Navigation Commission. Document C-WP/7809: *1818th Report to Council by the President of the Air Navigation Commission* (February 16, 1984).

————, Montreal, Executive Committee. Document 9409, A24-EX: *Executive Committee: Report and Minutes* (September–October 1983).

Jacob, Alain. "Circonstances atténuantes?" *Le Monde,* September 10, 1983.

Johnson, R. W. "007: Licence to Kill?" *The Guardian,* December 17, 1983.

Kahneman, Daniel, Paul Slovic, and Amos Tversky, eds. *Judgment Under Uncertainty: Heuristics and Biases.* Cambridge, England: Cambridge University Press, 1982.

Kenez, Peter. "How Moscow Handled the 007 Affair." *The New Leader,* October 31, 1983, pp. 10–12.

————. "The Lessons of 007." In Joseph Gordon, ed., *Psychological Operations, East and West.* Boulder, Colo.: Westview Press, 1985 (forthcoming).

Kennedy, William V., and S. Michael de Gyurky. "An Alternative Strategy for the 80's." *National Defense,* July/August 1983, pp. 47–54.

Klare, Michael. "Asia: Theatre of Nuclear War." *South* (London), no. 37 (November 1983), pp. 9–14.

Krepon, Michael, and Barry Blechman. "America's Global Lie Detector." *Popular Mechanics,* February 1984, pp. 86–89.

Kruzhin, Peter. "Severer Punishment for Military Offenses." Radio Liberty Research Publications, RL86/84, February 21, 1984.

Lambeth, Benjamin S. "Is Soviet Air Defense Fearsomely Inept?" *Los Angeles Times,* October 21, 1983.

Machado, François. "The Destruction of the KAL 007 (KE007)—How Did It Happen?" *ITA Magazine,* January 1984, pp. 15–30.

Mann, P. Q. (pseud.) "Reassessing the Sakhalin Incident." *Defence Attaché* (London), no. 3 (June 1984), pp. 41–56.

Ostrich, Ralph. "Aeroflot." *Armed Forces Journal International,* May 1981, pp. 38–56.

Park, Jae Kyu, and Joseph Ha, eds. *The Soviet Union and East Asia in the 1980s.* Boulder, Colo.: Westview Press, 1983.

Parker, Ron. "KAL 007." Unpublished undergraduate paper, Stanford University, January 1984.

Paul, Anthony. "Shot Down Over Russia! The Mysterious Saga of Flight 902." *Reader's Digest,* November 1978, pp. 138–44.

Pearson, David. "K.A.L. 007: What the U.S. Knew and When We Knew It." *The Nation,* August 18–25, 1984, pp. 105–24.

"Perception and Propaganda in the New Cold War: The Tragedy of Flight 007 and the Future of U.S.-Soviet Relations." Institute of International Studies, University of California, Berkeley, *Foreign Policy News Clips,* Vol. V, no. 5 (December 21, 1983).

Pfaff, William. "How U.S. Distorted Jet Crisis." *Los Angeles Times,* October 16, 1983.

Radio Free Europe/Radio Liberty, Soviet Area Audience and Opinion Research. "The Korean Airline Incident, Western Radio and Soviet Perceptions" (AR 4–84, April 1984).

Robbins, Christopher. *Air America.* New York: Putnam, 1979.

Rohmer, Richard. *Massacre 747.* Markham, Ont., Canada: PaperJacks, 1984.

Sampson, Anthony. "What Happened to Flight 007?" *Parade Magazine,* April 22, 1984, pp. 12–13.

Scheer, Robert. "Outrage Over the Korean Jet Can Mislead Us." *Los Angeles Times,* September 18, 1983.

Schmid, Karin. "Zum neuen Grenzgesetz der USSR." *Berichte* des Bundesinstituts für ostwissenschaftliche und internationale Studien (Köln), no. 18 (1984).

Sherwin, Lawrence. "The KAL Incident: Analysis of a Soviet Propaganda Campaign." Radio Liberty Research Publications, RL 371/83, October 4, 1983.

Soviet Armed Forces Review Annual. Vols. I–VII. Gulf Breeze, Fla.: Academic International Press, 1977–84.

"Soviets' Murderous Military Bungling." *Far Eastern Economic Review,* January 19, 1984.

Stephan, John J. "KAL 007 Through Soviet Eyes," *Honolulu Advertiser,* November 20, 1983.

Sych, Colonel V. "Signal prozvuchal noch'iu." *Krasnaia Zvezda,* October 16, 1983.

Tarasulo, Yitzhak. "Is Soviet Radar Really That Bad?" *Armed Forces Journal International,* February 1984, pp. 70–74.

Thames Television Ltd, London. "007—Licensed to Spy?" (July 19, 1984.)

Toth, Robert C. "Top Soviet Leadership Split, U.S. Experts Say." *Los Angeles Times,* October 3, 1983.

United Nations. Security Council. *Provisional Verbatim Record . . . ,* September 6–12, 1983.

Yanagida, Kunio. *Gekitsui.* Tokyo: Kodansha, 1984.

Index

Aeroflot, 11, 82
Afanas'yev, Viktor, 85
Afghanistan, 4, 6, 11, 13, 75, 89, 95, 103
Air Defense Command. *See* PVO
Air Rhodesia, 80
Aleutians, 9. *See also* Shemya Island
Anchorage, Alaska, 1, 17, 19, 26, 28, 29, 30, 32, 37, 39, 44*n*, 45, 46, 47, 49, 56, 108, 109, 113, 115, 116
Anderson, Jack, 112, 119
Andrews Air Force Base, 49
Andropov, Yuri, 5, 85–86, 92, 99, 120
Angola, 4
Armenia, 79, 119
AWACS, 51, 78

"Badger," 51
Barbados, 80
Belorussia, 75
Bendix, 29
Bering Strait, 59
Berlin, 44
Bessmertnykh, Aleksandr, 3
Bethel, Alaska, 17, 19, 32, 40, 46, 113
"Black box," ix, x, 25, 81, 105, 111
Boeing (also B707, B717, B747), 1, 17, 28, 35, 47, 49, 59, 60, 62, 79, 80–81, 101, 113
Bovin, Aleksandr, 61, 108
Brezhnev, Leonid, 5
Bulgaria, 79
Burt, Richard, 3, 93, 115

Cairo, 80
Canada, 11, 16, 73, 82

Carter, Jimmy, and Carter Administration, 4, 16
"Challenger," U.S. space shuttle, 51, 53, 55
Chernenko, Konstantin, 92
Chicago Convention (1944), 68, 91, 97, 122
China, 14, 76, 91
Chita, USSR, 64–65
Cho Choong Hoon, 27
Chukotka, 50, 77
Chun Byung In, 35, 37, 114–16
CIA. *See* United States government
Coral Sea. *See* U.S.S. Coral Sea
Corfu Channel, 67
CSA, 82
Cuba, 8, 78, 80, 82, 104
Cubaña Airlines, 82

Dayan, Moshe, 79
Decision-making, ix, 85–87, 92
Dolinsk-Sokol, 63
Duffy, Henry, 36

Eagleburger, Lawrence, 3, 93, 108
Eban, Abba, 79
EC-130, 79, 119
El Al Israel Airlines, 79, 120
Electronic intelligence, 4, 10, 12, 21, 47, 49–51, 53–54, 61, 75–76, 102, 110–11, 112, 119
El Salvador, 6
Enterprise. *See* U.S.S. Enterprise
Evans, Rowland, and Robert Novak, 10

F4-E, 79
"Flagon." *See* Sukhoi, Su-15
"Flogger." *See* MiG-23
France, 14
French sources, 38

Gabriel, Charles, 87
George, Alexander L., 95
Germany, 16, 73
Gotoda, Masaharu, 110
Govorov, Vladimir, 121
Great Circle route, 30–31, 37, 38, 40
Grishin, 85
Gromyko, Andrei, 3, 94*n*, 108
Groton, Connecticut, 82
GRU (Soviet military intelligence), 75
Guyana, 14

Hitler, Adolf, 71
Hokkaido, 1, 2, 19, 21, 30, 39, 40, 46, 59
Honduras, 6
Honshu, 19, 46
Hughes, William J., 67
Hyland, William G., 87

ICBM. *See* Missiles and missile tests
India, 91
Inertial Navigation System (INS), 28–30,
    32, 36, 43, 80
Inman, Bobby, 112
International Civil Aviation Organization
    (ICAO), 11, 14, 15, 30, 32, 34, 36,
    39, 41–42, 44, 58, 67–68, 91, 93, 97,
    108, 109, 115, 118, 122
International Court of Justice, 67
International Federation of Air Line Pilots
    Associations, 11, 36
International law, 66–69, 108, 118–19
Israel, 79–80, 120

Jackson-Vanik Amendment, 4
Jacob, Alain, 44*n*
Japan, 2, 3, 6, 13, 16, 17, 73, 76, 79, 107
Japan, Sea of, 3, 7, 40, 62, 119
Japanese Communist Party, 59
Japanese defense forces and intelligence,
    1, 2, 21, 25, 30, 38, 39, 102, 110–11
John Birch Society, 28, 107
Johnson, R. W., 42

KAL 007: flight and fate, 1, 2, 9, 17–25;
    human error hypotheses, 10, 27, 29–
    36, 55; intelligence hypotheses, 27,
    38, 40–55; lights, 7, 43, 44;

malfunction theories, 10, 27–29;
    search and rescue, 2, 3, 10–11, 25,
    111; willful action theories, 27, 36–
    40, 55
KAL 015, 19, 39, 45, 47
KAL 017, 100
KAL 902, 80–81, 98
Kalinin, USSR, 65
Kamchatka, 3, 4, 9, 15, 19, 21, 26, 27, 29,
    30, 37, 39–41, 44, 47, 53, 54, 56*n*,
    58, 60, 61, 62, 66, 69, 77, 79, 114,
    117, 118
Karaginski Island, 58
Karelia, 64
Kato, Yoshiya, 3
Keegan, George, 109, 114
Kem, USSR, 81
Kenai, 113
Keppel, John, 117
KGB (Committee on State Security), 65,
    75
Kiev, USSR, 5, 11
Kim Eui Dong, 35
Kimhae, 37
Kimpo International Airport. *See* Seoul
King Salmon, Alaska, 17, 19
Kirkpatrick, Jeane J., 10–13, 22, 103, 111
Kirsanov, Piotr, 15, 50, 116
Kissinger, Henry, 4, 120
Kola Peninsula, USSR, 45, 64, 81, 82, 112
Korea, North, 44
Korea, Republic of, 1, 2, 6, 35, 39, 41,
    109, 116
Korean Air Lines, 1, 2, 27, 32, 38, 45, 100,
    114–15, 116
Kornienko, Georgi, 14, 90
Kurile Islands, 21, 50, 59, 77
Kyodo, 2, 3, 110

LaPérouse Strait, 39, 77
Lebanon, 6, 75, 89
Lenin, Vladimir, 13
Libyan Airlines, 79–80
Linnik, Viktor, 117
Litton Aero Products, 28, 35
London, 79
LOT, 82
Lusitania, 67

Malta, 14
Maritime Province, Maritime Territory,
    50, 54
McDonald, Larry P., 28, 107, 112
Meir, Golda, 79
Mexico, 73
Midway. *See* U.S.S. Midway

MiG-15, 79, 120
MiG-23, 21, 66
Misawa, 46
Missiles and missile tests, 5, 10, 15–16, 25, 29, 49, 53–54, 56*n*, 58–59, 61, 64, 77, 84, 86, 99, 111
Moneron Island, 3, 107
Moskvitelev, Nikolai, 117
Murmansk Peninsula. *See* Kola Peninsula

NABIE, 17, 19, 47, 113
Narita International Airport. *See* Tokyo
Natsume, Haruo, 110
NEEVA, 17, 19, 37, 47, 113
Nemuro, 1
Netherlands, 14
New York, 1, 2, 5, 17, 100, 113, 115
Nicaragua, 6, 14, 75, 89
NINNO, 17
NIPPI, 19, 21, 113
Nixon, Richard M., 4, 112
Nkomo, Joshua, 80
NOKKA, 17, 19
Nuclear weapons, 5, 6, 96

Ogarkov, Nikolai, 14–15, 20, 21, 61, 64–65, 81, 85–87, 90, 91, 113, 114, 115
Okinawa, 111
Okhotsk, Sea of, 4, 19, 21, 26, 45, 50, 60, 66, 77
Olympics, 4, 116
Ovinnikov, Richard, 12

Pakistan, 14
Paris, 80
Pavlov, Vladimir, 3, 107
Pearson, David E., 48, 115
Petropavlovsk-on-Kamchatka, 20, 21, 60, 77, 116
Plesetsk, 53, 59
Poland, 14
Powers, Gary, 78, 84
"Provocation," 7, 9, 13, 89
PVO, Soviet air defense command and air defense forces, ix, 3, 9, 13, 15, 51, 58, 59, 63–66, 69, 83, 92, 96–97, 100, 103, 118

Radar, 1, 4, 7, 29, 30, 38, 39, 45, 59, 117
Radio Liberty, 92*n*
Ratmanova Island, 59
RC-135, 9, 19, 20, 47–48, 50, 51, 59, 61–62, 78, 94, 97, 101, 108, 117
Reagan, Ronald, 5, 6, 7, 8, 10, 11, 16, 61, 95, 103, 108, 119

Rohmer, Richard, 36–38, 109, 111, 118
Romanov, Semion F., 9, 115, 121

Sakhalin, 2, 3, 4, 7, 15, 19, 21, 26, 27, 29, 30, 37, 39, 40, 41, 44, 45, 46, 50, 54, 62–63, 66, 69, 77, 84, 87, 101, 102, 113–14, 118
SALT II Treaty, 4, 53
SAM-2, 61, 64, 114
Scheer, Robert, 80
Seoul, 1, 2, 17, 26, 30, 37, 39, 40, 80, 100, 108, 115, 116
Shemya Island, 20, 45, 47, 54, 58, 113, 115
Shultz, George P., 3, 4, 93, 107, 108, 111, 120
Siberia, 77
Simes, Dimitri, 94
Sokolov, Oleg, 3
Son Dong Hwi, 35
Sovetskaia Gavan', 77
Soviet interceptors, 3, 4, 21ff., 62–66, 87, 114, 118; lights and wings, 9; radio signals, 7, 9, 43, 66, 109, 114; warning shots, 7, 9, 15–16, 66
Soviet Union. *See* Union of Soviet Socialist Republics
Speakes, Larry, 110
SR-71, 44, 78, 115
SS-13, 53
SS-X-25, 53, 54
Stalin era, 72, 74
Stephan, John J., 72*n*
Sturua, Melor, 114
Sukhoi, Su-15, 21–25, 29, 62, 66, 81, 109
Sverdlovsk, 120

TASS, 2, 3, 6, 75
Tel Aviv, 79
Time zones, 1*n*
Togo, 14
Togo, Kazuhiko, 2
Tokyo, 2, 19, 29, 46, 109, 113
Troyanovsky, Oleg, 13, 15
Tsushima Strait, 77
Turkey, 79, 85
TVD (Theater of military operations), 63–66, 96, 121

U-2, 78, 84, 89, 104, 115, 120
Ukraine, 75
Union of Soviet Socialist Republics (USSR): Law on USSR State Borders, 13, 60, 65, 66–68, 118–19; Ministry of Civil Aviation, 69; Ministry of

Defense, 14; Ministry of Foreign
  Affairs, 2, 14; State Commission for
  Civil Aviation Safety, 14–15
United Nations, 8, 10–14, 21, 93, 94*n*,
  108
United States government, ix; Central
  Intelligence Agency (CIA), 2, 41,
  112–16, 119; Congress, 4, 11, 115;
  Department of Defense, 93, 100;
  Department of State, 2, 3, 4, 10, 15–
  16, 93, 108; intelligence activities, 9,
  40ff., 117; National Aeronautics and
  Space Administration (NASA), 29,
  116; National Security Agency
  (NSA), 22, 47, 48, 56, 111, 120;
  National Security Council (NSC), 6,
  8, 10, 95; United States Information
  Agency (USIA), 116; White House,
  10, 100, 110, 116

U.S.S. Coral Sea, 59
U.S.S. Enterprise, 59
U.S.S. Midway, 59

Vladivostok, 45, 54, 66, 77

Wakkanai, 21, 46, 111
Weinberger, Caspar, 10, 119
World War II, 71, 73, 74

Yuzhno-Sakhalinsk, 2, 114

Zaire, 14
Zamiatin, Leonid, 14, 90
Zimbabwe, 14, 80
Zimmerman, Warren, 3

Designer: Steve Renick
Compositor: Innovative Media, Inc.
Text: 10/12 Sabon (VIP)
Display: Helvetica
Printer: Braun-Brumfield, Inc.
Binder: Braun-Brumfield, Inc.